THE MYSTERY OF DUMSEY MEADOW

Music by David Perkins

Book and lyrics

by Caroline Dooley and David Perkins

SAMUEL FRENCH

samuelfrench.co.uk

Copyright © 2018 by Caroline Dooley and David Perkins
All Rights Reserved

THE MYSTERY OF DUMSEY MEADOW is fully protected under the copyright laws of the British Commonwealth, including Canada, the United States of America, and all other countries of the Copyright Union. All rights, including professional and amateur stage productions, recitation, lecturing, public reading, motion picture, radio broadcasting, television and the rights of translation into foreign languages are strictly reserved.

ISBN 978-0-573-11525-7

www.samuelfrench.co.uk

www.samuelfrench.com

For Amateur Production Enquiries

United Kingdom and World
excluding North America
plays@samuelfrench.co.uk
020 7255 4302/01

Each title is subject to availability from Samuel French, depending upon country of performance.

CAUTION: Professional and amateur producers are hereby warned that *THE MYSTERY OF DUMSEY MEADOW* is subject to a licensing fee. Publication of this play does not imply availability for performance. Both amateurs and professionals considering a production are strongly advised to apply to the appropriate agent before starting rehearsals, advertising, or booking a theatre. A licensing fee must be paid whether the title is presented for charity or gain and whether or not admission is charged.

No one shall make any changes in this title for the purpose of production. No part of this book may be reproduced, stored in a retrieval system, or transmitted in any form, by any means, now known or yet to be invented, including mechanical, electronic, photocopying, recording, videotaping, or otherwise, without the prior written permission of the publisher. No one shall upload this title, or part of this title, to any social media websites.

The right of Caroline Dooley and David Perkins to be identified as authors of this work has been asserted in accordance with Section 77 of the Copyright, Designs and Patents Act 1988.

THINKING ABOUT PERFORMING A SHOW?

There are thousands of plays and musicals available to perform from Samuel French right now, and applying for a licence is easier and more affordable than you might think

---

From classic plays to brand new musicals, from monologues to epic dramas, there are shows for everyone.

Plays and musicals are protected by copyright law so if you want to perform them, the first thing you'll need is a licence. This simple process helps support the playwright by ensuring they get paid for their work, and means that you'll have the documents you need to stage the show in public.

Not all our shows are available to perform all the time, so it's important to check and apply for a licence before you start rehearsals or commit to doing the show.

LEARN MORE & FIND THOUSANDS OF SHOWS

Browse our full range of plays and musicals and find out more about how to license a show

www.samuelfrench.co.uk/perform

Talk to the friendly experts in our Licensing team for advice on choosing a show, and help with licensing

plays@samuelfrench.co.uk   020 7387 9373

Acting Editions
BORN TO PERFORM

Playscripts designed from the ground up to work the way you do in rehearsal, performance and study

---

Larger, clearer text for easier reading

Wider margins for notes

Performance features such as character and props lists, sound and lighting cues, and more

---

+ CHOOSE A SIZE AND STYLE TO SUIT YOU

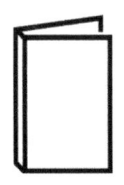

STANDARD EDITION
Our regular paperback book at our regular size

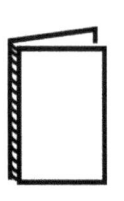

SPIRAL-BOUND EDITION
The same size as the Standard Edition, but with a sturdy, easy-to-fold, easy-to-hold spiral-bound spine

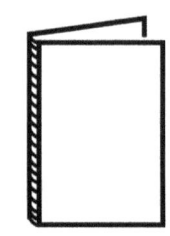

LARGE EDITION
A4 size and spiral bound, with larger text and a blank page for notes opposite every page of text. Perfect for technical and directing use

---

| LEARN MORE | samuelfrench.co.uk/actingeditions |

**Other musicals by CAROLINE DOOLEY
AND DAVID PERKINS
published by Samuel French**

The Happy Prince

The Selfish Giant

**Other musicals by DAVID PERKINS
published by Samuel French**

The Curious Quest for the Sandman's Sand

The Nutcracker

Shake, Ripple & Roll

Skool & Crossbones

Pandemonium! (a Greek Myth-adventure)

**FIND PERFECT PLAYS TO PERFORM AT
www.samuelfrench.co.uk/perform**

ABOUT THE AUTHORS

CAROLINE DOOLEY has worked in many areas of the performing arts as an actor, administrator, teacher and writer. She performed Theatre-in-Education shows and 'History Alive' workshops in schools and ran after-school drama clubs for many years. She writes for and performs in a comedy cabaret duo and leads weekly drama classes for adults. She has collaborated with David Perkins on two other musicals, *The Selfish Giant* and *The Happy Prince*, also published by Samuel French.

DAVID PERKINS works as a composer, pianist, musical director and music arranger. Published works include *Shake, Ripple & Roll, Pandemonium! (a Greek Myth-adventure), The Nutcracker and Skool & Crossbones* with lyricist Jenifer Toksvig; and adaptations of *The Selfish Giant* and *The Happy Prince* with Caroline Dooley. All of David's musicals have received their premiere performances at Guildford's Yvonne Arnaud Youth Theatre, where he is also the musical director.

IMPORTANT INFORMATION

Alterations to the script and score

If changes, additions or cuts to the show are required to make it work for a particular group, any proposed alterations (no matter how small) MUST be approved by the authors before rehearsals commence. Approval can be sought via Samuel French Ltd or directly from the authors via email: **david.perkins@dp-music.co.uk**

The authors are happy to provide suggestions for such things as cuts, scene change music, chorus character names and so on. Making contact with them is easy and they will consider any request. Making small changes this way is free of charge and it turns an illegal alteration into a legal one.

Video and audio recordings

In certain circumstances, permission may be given for a video or audio recording of your show to be made. Please apply to Samuel French Ltd for full details. Video and audio recordings made without prior permission are STRICTLY not allowed, even for archival or training purposes.

THE MYSTERY OF DUMSEY MEADOW

First performed at the Yvonne Arnaud Theatre, Guildford, UK on 7th December 2006 by the Yvonne Arnaud Youth Theatre ACT 2 with the following cast:

FARMER BILL	Phelim Brady
MISS FEATHERSTONE	Felicity Sturge
GERALDINE	Beth Finney
SYLVIA	Jessica McCabe
MILLY	Tilly-Jane Wilson
MR NOBLE	Michael Cotton
JENNINGS	Josh Freeborn
PORTER	Guy Peters
ALEC	Jack Sunderland
LADY DUMSEY	Shayna Layton
MARY/HOODED WOMAN	Maddie Winn
PC GREEN	Matthew Sharman-Hayles
VICAR	Luke Hornsby-Smith
DOROTHEA	Sascha Causton
AGNES	Harriet Smithers
JOURNALIST	Nick Viera

St Winifred's School:
Beth Finney, Jessica McCabe, Tilly-Jane Wilson, Claire Lowrey, Emily Andrews, Anna Anderson, Kate Burgess, Megan Golder, Charlotte Payne, Helen Jones, Maddie Winn

St Albert's School:
Josh Freeborn, Guy Peters, Jack Sunderland, Chris Clark, Jack Nicole, Nicholas Beesley, Cameron Manson, Nick Viera

Production Team
Directed by Julia Black
Musical direction by David Perkins
Set and lighting design by Sharon Davey

CHARACTERS

LADY DUMSEY
FARMER BILL
PC GREEN
VICAR
DOROTHEA
AGNES
MARY / HOODED WOMAN
JOURNALIST
MISS FEATHERSTONE
MILLY*
GERALDINE*
SYLVIA*
PERKINS
MR NOBLE
ALEC**
JENNINGS**
PORTER**
**THE CHILDREN OF ST WINIFRED'S
& ST ALBERT'S SCHOOLS**

* Named pupils from St Winifred's School
** Named pupils from St Albert's School

CHARACTER DESCRIPTIONS

Seventeen named parts (8m, 8f, 1m/f) + flexible chorus (see note on page xv)

LADY DUMSEY (f) — Lady of the Manor and owner of the Dumsey Estate. She is posh and slightly eccentric.
SONGS: *The Mystery of Dumsey Meadow* (solo), *Things to Do* (solo), *How Thrilling!* (Reprise #2) (solo), Bows/Encore

FARMER BILL (m) — The farmer on the Dumsey Estate. He is very jolly and is often singing because he is, in fact, slightly tipsy. This should not be overplayed as the audience must not be aware that he is actually drunk.
SONGS: *The Gladness of the May* (solo), *Things to Do* (solo), *The Gladness of the May* (Reprise), *How Thrilling!* (Reprise #2), Bows/Encore

PC GREEN (m) — The local policeman. He is efficient, keen to help and proud to be a *Bobby on the Beat*.
SONGS: *Bobby on the Beat* (solo), *The Physical Contest* (solo), *The Practical Contest*, *How Thrilling!* (Reprise #2) (solo), Bows/Encore

VICAR (m) — The local vicar. He is polite and courteous.
SONGS: *Witches are Bewitching* (solo), *The Physical Contest*, *The Practical Contest* (solo), *How Thrilling!* (Reprise #2) (solo), Bows/Encore

DOROTHEA AND AGNES (f)	Mysterious and slightly scary elderly sisters with a habit of speaking in rhyme. **SONGS:** *Sisters of Rhyme* (solos), *Sisters of Rhyme* (Encore #1) (solos), *Sisters of Rhyme* (Encore #2) (solos), *How Thrilling!* (Reprise #2), Bows/Encore
MARY/HOODED WOMAN (f)	Played by the same person. Mary is the Vicar's wife, who appears throughout the play dressed up as a hooded woman. The audience must not know that the Hooded Woman is actually Mary until the final scene. **SONGS:** *How Thrilling!* (Reprise #2) (solo), Bows/Encore
JOURNALIST (m/f)	A journalist from the *Daily Herald*. S/he is pushy and unscrupulous, stopping at nothing to get a good story. **SONGS:** *How Thrilling!* (Reprise #2), Bows/Encore

St Winifred's School:

MISS FEATHERSTONE (f)	An experienced teacher. She is prim and proper, with high standards for her girls. **SONGS:** *How Thrilling!* (solo), *The Mystery of Dumsey Meadow*, *The Physical Contest*, *The Practical Contest* (solo), *How Thrilling!* (Reprise #2), Bows/Encore
MILLY (f)	The smallest and cleverest child in St Winifred's School. She is often picked on by the other girls but always manages to rise above it.

	SONGS: *How Thrilling!*, *Re-Entrance of St Winnie's*, *The Mystery of Dumsey Meadow*, *Sisters of Rhyme* (solo), *Sisters of Rhyme* (Encore #1) (solo), *Sisters of Rhyme* (Encore #2) (solo), *I'd Rather Have Brains Than Brawn* (solo), *How Thrilling!* (Reprise #2), Bows/Encore
GERALDINE (f)	The Head Girl of St Winifred's. She is outwardly virtuous but secretly sly and calculating. **SONGS:** *How Thrilling!*, *Re-Entrance of St Winnie's*, *The Mystery of Dumsey Meadow*, *How Thrilling!* (Reprise #1), *Bobby on the Beat* (solo), *The Physical Contest, The Practical Contest* (solo), *The Tea-Break Tie-Break*, *How Thrilling!* (Reprise #2), Bows/Encore
SYLVIA (f)	She is Geraldine's sidekick and although in her shadow, she is every bit as calculating. **SONGS:** *How Thrilling!* (solo), *Re-Entrance of St Winnie's*, *The Mystery of Dumsey Meadow*, *How Thrilling!* (Reprise #1), *Bobby on the Beat* (solo), The Physical Contest, *The Practical Contest*, *The Tea-Break Tie-Break*, *How Thrilling!* (Reprise #2), Bows/Encore
PERKINS (m)	The elderly school driver and general factotum. He is constantly put upon with tasks that he wearily and begrudgingly carries out.

                    SONGS: *How Thrilling!* (Reprise #2), Bows/Encore

CHILDREN (SW)   The well-behaved girls of St Winifred's School (see note on page xv).
                    SONGS: *How Thrilling!, Re-Entrance of St Winnie's, The Mystery of Dumsey Meadow, How Thrilling!* (Reprise #1), *Bobby on the Beat, The Physical Contest, The Practical Contest, The Tea-Break Tie-Break, How Thrilling!* (Reprise #2), Bows/Encore

St Albert's School:

MR NOBLE (m)   A recently qualified and inexperienced teacher. He is unable to control his class of children and is in awe of Miss Featherstone.
                    SONGS: *The Mystery of Dumsey Meadow, The Physical Contest* (solo), *The Practical Contest, How Thrilling!* (Reprise #2), Bows/Encore

ALEC (m)   The smallest and cleverest child in the school. He is bullied and constantly picked on, which he generally ignores.
                    SONGS: *St Albert's School Motto, The Mystery of Dumsey Meadow, Witches are Bewitching* (solo), *I'd Rather Have Brains Than Brawn* (solo), *The Gladness of the May* (Reprise), *How Thrilling!* (Reprise #2), Bows/Encore

JENNINGS (m) — The Head Boy of St Albert's. He thinks he's superior to everyone, especially his superiors.
SONGS: *St Albert's School Motto, The Mystery of Dumsey Meadow, How Thrilling!* (Reprise #1), *Witches are Bewitching* (solo), *The Physical Contest, The Practical Contest* (solo), *The Tea-Break Tie-Break, How Thrilling!* (Reprise #2), Bows/Encore

PORTER (m) — Jennings's sidekick. He is a liar and a bully.
SONGS: *St Albert's School Motto, The Mystery of Dumsey Meadow, How Thrilling!* (Reprise #1), *Witches are Bewitching* (solo), *The Physical Contest, The Practical Contest, The Tea-Break Tie-Break, How Thrilling!* (Reprise #2), Bows/Encore

CHILDREN (SA) — The badly-behaved pupils of St Albert's School (see note on page xv)
SONGS: *St Albert's School Motto, The Mystery of Dumsey Meadow, How Thrilling!* (Reprise #1), *Witches are Bewitching, The Physical Contest, The Practical Contest, The Tea-Break Tie-Break, How Thrilling!* (Reprise #2), Bows/Encore

A NOTE ABOUT THE CHILDREN

In an ideal scenario, the children of St Winifred's School would be played by girls and the children of St Albert's School by boys. If this is not possible, then the following options are permissible in order of preference:

(i)
St Winifred's   Girls
St Albert's   A mixture of boys and girls, the boys having the named roles

(ii)
St Winifred's   Girls
St Albert's   Girls playing the characters as boys

(iii)
St Winifred's   Girls
St Albert's   Girls playing the characters as girls

In the case of (iii), the part of Alec should be changed to Alex throughout the play and pronouns altered accordingly.

EXTRA DIALOGUE FOR CHILDREN

Throughout the script there are a number of lines spoken by individual, unnamed children. If this is not sufficient for the numbers involved, an idea for extra dialogue can be found on page 81.

SET

Although the play is divided up into various scenes, all the action can take place on one single set – a countryside setting suggesting rural England in the 1930s. The main area of the stage should represent Dumsey Meadow itself, mainly grass and perhaps an apple tree (referred to in the script). Other locations on the Dumsey Estate could be to the side of the main area, using additional pieces of scenery, e.g. a five-bar gate, signpost etc. or the main area could be used with lighting to suggest a different place.

COSTUMES

All the costumes, wherever possible, should reflect England in the 1930s. The St Winifred's school uniform should be smart and the pupils neat and well-presented at all times. The St Albert's school pupils also wear uniforms but, due to a lack of discipline in their school, tend to look rather scruffy. All the other characters in the play should wear costumes that reflect their personalities or occupation in a simple, obvious and perhaps archetypal way.

FURNITURE AND PROPERTIES

A list of furniture and properties can be found on page 83. Many are essential to the show and can be as simple or elaborate as resources allow. Others can be added at the discretion of the director.

LIGHTING

Great effects and atmosphere can be achieved through lighting and, if used thoughtfully, it can reduce the need for elaborate scenery. The ability to isolate individual areas of the stage with the creative use of "specials", stage "washes", follow-spots and "gobos" will add a great deal to the performance and the audience's enjoyment.

INSTRUMENTATION

Band parts available on hire from Samuel French Ltd

Piano
Flute doubling Clarinet in Bb (or part shared by 2 players)
Double Bass
Drums/Percussion
The show can be performed with just a piano accompaniment or with any combination of the above instruments.

BACKING TRACKS

Available on hire from Samuel French Ltd

If the performance of the music using live musicians is not an option, then a CD containing all the necessary tracks including transitional music and sound effects can be hired from Samuel French. A backing track plot can be found on page 86.

SOUND EFFECTS

A sound effects plot can be found on page 84. A CD containing these important effects can be obtained from Samuel French Ltd.

SCENES

The play is set in the heart of the English countryside in the year 1938. The action takes place in Dumsey Meadow and at unspecified outdoor locations around the Dumsey Estate.

Prologue — *Somewhere on the Dumsey Estate*
Farmer Bill

Scene One – Arrivals and Rivals — *Dumsey Meadow*
Children, Mr Noble, Miss Featherstone, Perkins, Lady Dumsey, Dorothea, Agnes

Scene Two – Meetings and Greetings — *Somewhere on the Dumsey Estate*
Hooded Woman, PC Green, Vicar, Mr Noble, Miss Featherstone, Perkins, Dorothea, Agnes

Scene Three – Witches and Warnings — *Dumsey Meadow*
Children (SA), PC Green, Vicar, Farmer Bill, Journalist, Hooded Woman

Scene Four – Law and Order — *Dumsey Meadow*
Journalist, Children (SW), PC Green

Scene Five – Reason and Rhyme — *Somewhere on the Dumsey Estate*
Lady Dumsey, Vicar, Milly, Farmer Bill, Alec, Journalist, Hooded Woman, Dorothea, Agnes

Scene Six – The Battle Begins *Dumsey Meadow*
Children (except Alec), Mr Noble, Miss Featherstone, Perkins, PC Green, Vicar

Scene Seven – A Meeting of Minds *Somewhere on the Dumsey Estate*
Milly, Alec

Scene Eight – War and Peace *Dumsey Meadow*
Company

DURATION

1 hour 20 minutes (approx.) with an optional interval in Scene Five, page 45

MUSICAL NUMBERS

"Overture" – a spring morning in the English Countryside
(Effects 1, see page 84)

1	**The Gladness of the May**	Farmer Bill
2	**How Thrilling!**	Miss Featherstone, Sylvia, Children (SW)
2a	St Albert's School Motto	Children (SA)
2b	Re-Entrance of St Winnie's	Children (SW)
3	**The Mystery of Dumsey Meadow**	Lady Dumsey, Mr Noble, Miss Featherstone, Children
3a	How Thrilling! (Reprise #1)	Children (not Alec/Milly)
3b	Scene Change / Appearance of Hooded Woman	
3c	Scene Change	
4	**Witches are Bewitching**	Vicar, Alec, Jennings, Porter, Children (SA)
5	**Bobby on the Beat**	PC Green, Geraldine, Sylvia, Children (SW) (not Milly)
5a	Scene Change	
6	**Things to Do**	Lady Dumsey, Farmer Bill
6a	Appearance of Hooded Woman	
7	**Sisters of Rhyme**	Milly, Dorothea, Agnes
7a	Sisters of Rhyme (Encore #1)	Milly, Dorothea, Agnes
7b	Sisters of Rhyme (Encore #2)	Milly, Dorothea, Agnes

7c	Scene Change	
8	**The Physical Contest**	Mr Noble, Miss Featherstone, PC Green, Vicar, Children (not Alec/Milly)
8a	Scene Change	
9	**I'd Rather Have Brains Than Brawn**	Alec, Milly
10	**The Practical Contest**	Miss Featherstone, Mr Noble, Vicar, PC Green, Geraldine, Jennings, Children (not Alec/Milly)
10a	The Tea-Break Tie-Break	Children (not Alec/Milly)
10b	The Gladness of the May (Reprise)	Farmer Bill, Alec
10c	Appearance of Hooded Woman	
10d	Incidental	
11	**How Thrilling! (Reprise #2)**	Company
11a	Bows / Encore	Company
11b	Exit	

ACKNOWLEDGEMENTS

The authors would like to thank the following people:

Julia Black
Adam Forde
Tilly-Mae Millbrook
The 2008 Samuel French team: Vivien Goodwin, Amanda Smith and Sue Griffiths
The YAT Youth Theatre kids (and their parents)
and
The cows that graze on the banks of the River Thames in the *real* Dumsey Meadow

*Dedicated with gratitude to our parents
Anita, Ben, Mavis and Terry
for never taking us camping.*

The play is set in and around the Dumsey Estate in the heart of the English countryside. The year is 1938, it is May.

As the audience arrive we hear an "overture" of sounds – crows crowing, the dawn chorus chorusing and a cock-a-doodle do-ing (Effects 1).

Prologue
Somewhere on the Dumsey Estate

*It is early morning. We hear the sound of distant music (Music 1) – a simple clarinet. The **FARMER** starts to sing from off-stage. The country sound effects (Effects 1) slowly fade to nothing.*

SONG 1: "THE GLADNESS OF THE MAY" – Farmer Bill

FARMER BILL
THE SUN HAS RISEN ON A BRIGHT NEW DAY

FA LA LA LA
FA LA LA LA

FARMER BILL *enters carrying a Thermos flask. He is more cheerful than usual. Unbeknownst to the audience, he is in fact slightly tipsy, but it is important that he doesn't behave like a stage "drunk". To the audience he seems very merry...*

THE SUN HAS RISEN ON A BRIGHT NEW DAY
THE BIRDS ARE FULL OF SONG
THERE'S WORK TO DO BUT I DON'T CARE

I WILL SPEND MY DAY I'M NOT SURE WHERE
'TIL EVENING COMES ALONG

A sound effect of a crazy cow interrupts the song (Effects 2). The **FARMER** *looks surprised at the sound then continues his song.*

THE SUN HAS RISEN ON A BRIGHT NEW DAY
MY HEART IS FULL OF JOY
I'D LIKE TO SKIP AND RUN AND PLAY
AND "FEEL THE GLADNESS OF THE MAY!"
JUST LIKE A LOVESICK BOY

A sound effect of a crazy sheep interrupts the song (Effects 3). The **FARMER** *looks concerned then continues his song.*

THE SUN HAS RISEN ON A BRIGHT NEW DAY
THE—

An offstage, witch-like cackle alarms him (Effects 4), stops the song dead in its tracks and he exits hastily.

Scene One – Arrivals and Rivals
Dumsey Meadow

Music 2 starts.

A group of well-behaved **CHILDREN FROM ST WINIFRED'S SCHOOL** *enter, followed by their enthusiastic and energetic teacher,* **MISS FEATHERSTONE,** *who is studying a map and sporting a sensible rucksack.* **PERKINS** *the school driver staggers on behind them, laden down with tents and other camping equipment. The girls are clearly very excited about being on 'a jolly' in the countryside.*

MISS FEATHERSTONE Wait a minute please girls, I need to study the map.

She studies the map with great concentration.

The **CHILDREN** *revel in the fresh air and the prospect of their camping trip.*

SONG 2. "HOW THRILLING!" – Miss Featherstone, Sylvia, Children (SW)

CHILDREN (SW)
A CAMPING TRIP IS SUCH GOOD FUN
THE HIGHLIGHT OF OUR YEAR
FAREWELL TO BOOKS AND CLASSROOMS
NO LESSONS FOR A WEEK
NO ALGEBRA OR GREEK

A JOLLY TIME FOR EVERYONE
SO GLAD THAT WE ARE HERE
ALERT AND ALWAYS WILLING
FOR IT REALLY IS SO ABSOLUTELY THRILLING

HOW THRILLING
HOW THRILLING
IT REALLY IS SO ABSOLUTELY THRILLING
EXCITING!

INVITING!
A CAMPING TRIP FOR FIVE WHOLE DAYS
WE'LL HAVE SUCH FUN

SYLVIA *(spoken)* AND DADDY PAYS!

CHILDREN (SW) *(sung)*
HOW SPIFFING
HOW RIPPING
ONE COULD REMARK THIS CAMPING LARK IS GRIPPING
THEY THINK IT'S EDUCATIONAL
BUT WE THINK IT'S SENSATIONAL
HOW SPIFFING

MISS FEATHERSTONE
THE MOST IMPORTANT THING TO BEAR IN MIND
WHEN FACED WITH AN ADVENTURE OF THIS KIND
IS DON'T FORGET YOUR COMMON SENSE
WHEN LIGHTING FIRES AND PITCHING TENTS
FOR IF YOU DO YOU'LL SURELY FIND
THAT YOU WILL QUICKLY FALL BEHIND
AND THAT WOULD BE A SHAME
YOU MUST UPHOLD ST WINNIE'S NAME!

CHILDREN (SW)
HOW SPIFFING
HOW RIPPING
ONE COULD REMARK THIS CAMPING LARK IS GRIPPING

GROUP 1
THEY THINK IT'S EDUCATIONAL
BUT WE THINK IT'S SENSATIONAL

GROUP 2
WE'LL STAY UP LATE, HAVE MIDNIGHT FEASTS
AND FIGHT OFF LOTS OF SCARY BEASTS

GROUP 3
WE'RE SUPER FIT, WE'LL MAKE THE GRADE
AND PROVE THAT WE ARE NOT AFRAID

CHILDREN (SW)
IT REALLY IS SO ABSOLUTELY THRILLING!

SCENE ONE – ARRIVALS AND RIVALS

MISS FEATHERSTONE Thank you girls, that's quite enough. Now, open your lungs and breathe in this wonderful fresh air.

They all take a breath then exhale in disgust.

SYLVIA It smells jolly awful, if you ask me.

MISS FEATHERSTONE Thank you Sylvia, I didn't.

Music 2 continues as underscore.

We will now sing the St Winifred's School camping hymn, penned by the near-immortal St Winifred herself after a week's hardship on the Llanfydi campsite in the Brecon Beacons in 1864. Stand up straight and tall please.

They stand up straight and tall.

All together now…

CHILDREN (SW)
WITH CHIN HELD HIGH THROUGH SUN AND RAIN
OUR SPIRIT SHALL NOT WAIVER
THE TENT MAY LEAK BUT DON'T COMPLAIN
AND BE KIND TO YOUR NEIGHBOUR

MISS FEATHERSTONE Jolly good. And now our school motto girls…

Music 2 continues (unaccompanied).

CHILDREN (SW)
ADVENTURA EST VITAE ESSENTIAL ET AUDENTES FORTUNA JUVAT

[ad-ven-tour-ah est vee-tie es-sen-tee-al et ow-den-tays для-too-nah yoo-vat]

[ad-ven-tour-ah est vee-tie es-sen-tee-al et ow-den-tays for-too-nah yoo-vat]

MISS FEATHERSTONE Which means in translation?

MILLY, *the smallest and cleverest child in the school, puts her hand up.*

MILLY *(stepping forward)* Adventure is the essence of—

All the **CHILDREN** *turn to look at* **MILLY** *in disbelief that she has spoken, as this is the Head Girl's role.*

SYLVIA Not you, Milly!

MISS FEATHERSTONE *(throws* **MILLY** *a disapproving glance, then pointedly)* Geraldine...

GERALDINE Adventure is the essence of life and fortune favours the bold, Miss Featherstone.

Music 2 continues as underscore.

MISS FEATHERSTONE Very good, Geraldine Forster-Smythe, we're not Head Girl for nothing, are we? Come along girls, let's go and find Dumsey Meadow. Perkins can't wait to put up our tents, can you, Perkins?

PERKINS *(miserably)* No, Miss Featherstone.

MISS FEATHERSTONE Have you got all our bits and bobs?

PERKINS I believe this is just the *first* load, Miss Featherstone.

MISS FEATHERSTONE Well you'd better get on then. Come along everyone. Onward, ever onward and carpe diem! *[car-pay dee-em]*

The girls follow **MISS FEATHERSTONE** *off, singing as they go.* **PERKINS** *picks up the camping equipment and staggers off after them.*

CHILDREN (SW)
 IT REALLY, REALLY, REALLY IS
 IT REALLY, REALLY, REALLY IS
 IT REALLY IS SO ASBSOLUTELY THRILLING!

A group of ill-disciplined **CHILDREN FROM ST ALBERT'S SCHOOL** *enter with their inexperienced teacher,* **MR NOBLE**, *who is looking at a newspaper cutting. They are laden down with tents and lots of camping paraphernalia.* **ALEC**, *the smallest and cleverest child in the school, is wearing spectacles and is closely studying a map.*

SCENE ONE – ARRIVALS AND RIVALS

MR NOBLE Put your things down, everyone, while I study the picture. This might be the campsite.

The **CHILDREN** *put down their rucksacks, tents, kit bags etc.*

MR NOBLE *studies the picture in the article and looks around, comparing it with their surroundings.*

JENNINGS What are you looking for, Sir?

MR NOBLE Dumsey Meadow…which in the picture has a large apple tree in one corner.

JENNINGS *(pointing off into the distance, not at the apple tree)* There's an apple tree, Sir.

ALEC That's not an apple tree, it's an oak tree.

PORTER *(aside to* **ALEC***)* Who asked you, squirt?

MR NOBLE As Head Boy, Jennings, you should know that. Have you learnt nothing at St Albert's School?

JENNINGS *(sweetly)* Yes, Sir, of course Sir. *(loudly)* Come on, let's tell him.

Music 2a (unaccompanied).

CHILDREN (SA) *(chanted)*
ST ALBERT'S IS THE BEST, BEST, BEST
FAR BETTER THAN THE REST, REST, REST
ST ALBERT'S SCHOOL IS GREAT, GREAT, GREAT!

MR NOBLE That's enough! Right, St Albert's, prove you're the best. Help me find this meadow.

ALEC *(pointing)* There's an apple tree over there, Sir, and according to my map—

PORTER *(snatching map from* **ALEC***)* According to *my* map, Sir, I think we're in Dumsey Meadow already. *(pointing at the apple tree)* There's the apple tree.

MR NOBLE *(snatching the map from him)* Where did you get that map from, Porter?

PORTER Er...I found it lying on the ground, Sir...over there.

MR NOBLE If I find out that's a lie, I'll report you to the Headmaster and you'll never come on another camping trip. Do you understand?

PORTER Yes, Sir. *(cheekily)* But it's not, so you won't, and I will.

MR NOBLE *(exasperated)* Just wait here.

> **MR NOBLE** *sighs an exasperated sigh, opens up the map and storms off in cross pursuit of their meadow.*

JENNINGS You lying little toad, Porter. I saw you nick it from Carter. You're lucky I didn't tell on you.

PORTER Why's Four Eyes got a map anyway? He's such a creep.

JENNINGS Yes, Alec Carter, you're a creep.

CHILDREN (SA) *(all pointing at* **ALEC** *and speaking in unison)* Creep!

PORTER What's so great about camping anyway? It stinks round here.

JENNINGS That's the countryside for you.

ALEC No, he's right. There is a peculiar smell, but I'm not sure what it is yet.

> *He inhales deeply and tries hard to recognise the smell.*

PORTER I know exactly what it is, Carter. It's you!

CHILDREN (SA) *(chanting in unison)* Carter smells! Carter smells!

> *Music 2b starts as underscore.*

JENNINGS Quick everyone, someone's coming. Hide!

SCENE ONE – ARRIVALS AND RIVALS

The **ST ALBERT'S CHILDREN** *disperse around the stage and "hide". The* **ST WINIFRED'S CHILDREN** *re-enter with* **MISS FEATHERSTONE**, *followed by the increasingly weary* **PERKINS**, *still heavily laden.*

SONG 2b. "RE-ENTRANCE OF ST WINNIE'S" – Children (SW)

CHILDREN (SW)
IT REALLY, REALLY, REALLY IS
IT REALLY, REALLY, REALLY IS
IT REALLY IS SO ABSOLUTELY THRILLING!

MISS FEATHERSTONE Well, children, here we are – Dumsey Meadow.

The **CHILDREN** *look around excitedly.*

MR NOBLE *re-enters.*

MR NOBLE *(still grappling with the map which is fully opened and right in front of his face so that he doesn't notice the* **ST ALBERT'S CHILDREN** *are "in hiding")* Alright, everyone. Porter was right, this is definitely Dumsey—

MR NOBLE *lowers the map and sees the* **ST WINIFRED'S CHILDREN.**

Oh, hello!

JENNINGS *(coming out from his hiding place)* Come on, everyone. Looks like trouble.

JENNINGS *gestures to the other* **ST ALBERT'S CHILDREN** *and they emerge from their hiding places. A gasp from the* **ST WINIFRED'S CHILDREN** *and a tableau moment when all the* **CHILDREN**, **MR NOBLE** *and* **MISS FEATHERSTONE** *realise that they have company.*

MISS FEATHERSTONE *(offering to shake hands with the* **ST ALBERT'S TEACHER**, *which he does)* Good morning, my name is Miss Featherstone and we are from St Winifred's

School. I assume from your...paraphernalia that you are intending to camp here?

MR NOBLE Well...er...yes, that was the plan.

CHILDREN (SA) Yes!

MISS FEATHERSTONE Well, there must be some mistake. I made our booking a long time ago.

CHILDREN (SW) Yes!

MR NOBLE I'm sorry, Miss Weather—

MISS FEATHERSTONE *(curtly)* Feather—

MR NOBLE *(embarrassed)* I'm sorry, Miss *Feather*stone...but I'm rather new to all of this—

MISS FEATHERSTONE No need to apologise. We can't all have my vast breadth of experience.

The **ST WINIFRED'S CHILDREN** *snigger.*

Do continue.

MR NOBLE I don't know what to say really, except that St Albert's are meant to be here too, so...it seems we have a problem.

MISS FEATHERSTONE Indeed Mr—?

MR NOBLE Noble. Kenneth Noble.

PORTER *(aside)* Or Nobby, to his friends.

The **ST ALBERT'S CHILDREN** *snigger.*

GERALDINE Well, Mr Nobby, we Winnies aren't going to take this lying down. Are we, girls?

CHILDREN (SW) No, we're not. *(tossing their heads indignantly)* Hmmnn!

MISS FEATHERSTONE That appears to be settled then.

JENNINGS I don't think it is, Miss Featherduster. Come on, let's tell her.

SCENE ONE – ARRIVALS AND RIVALS

CHILDREN (SA) *(unaccompanied chant, as Music 2a)*
ST ALBERT'S IS THE BEST, BEST, BEST
FAR BETTER THAN THE REST, REST, REST
ST ALBERT'S SCHOOL IS GREAT, GREAT, GREAT!

The **ST WINIFRED'S CHILDREN** *retort angrily and a verbal battle ensues. The* **TEACHERS** *try to calm the* **CHILDREN** *down but they are so cross that a fight almost breaks out.*

LADY DUMSEY *enters to see what all the commotion is about. She is an eccentric woman with a vague manner. She carries a shotgun, which she aims into the sky and shoots (Effects 5). There is a stunned silence.*

LADY DUMSEY *(slightly flustered by what she has done)* Right... well...there we are. Dear, oh dear. What a noise. I'm Lady Dumsey, I own this meadow and I'd like to know what on earth is going on. Would somebody please care to explain?

The **CHILDREN** *all start to shout at once, each stating their right to be in the meadow.*

She shoots another shot into the air. (Effects 6)

Goodness me, children these days. Don't they teach you manners at school anymore?

ALEC I think there's been a double-booking.

MILLY We're all meant to be here.

LADY DUMSEY Well you can't all stay, there isn't room. I'm sorry. Since the apple harvest "mysteriously" failed last year I've been strapped for cash. I couldn't afford to keep my secretary on, which is why there's been a mistake. *(sighing self-pityingly)* This would never have happened if Peggy were still with me.

MISS FEATHERSTONE Let's not cry over spilt milk, Lady Dumsey. Our booking was confirmed and we Winnies intend to stay.

MR NOBLE *(bravely standing up to* **MISS FEATHERSTONE***)* But St Albert's is booked in too.

LADY DUMSEY Oh dear, what a year. I didn't want to turn my beautiful meadow into a campsite, I was forced to – the apples mysteriously rotted on the trees. I didn't sell a single one. It ruined me. And now a double-booking, oh dear. And how will I cope with all the other "strange and mysterious" things that are going on around here?

MILLY What other "strange and mysterious" things, Lady Dumsey?

GERALDINE *(nastily)* Be quiet, Milly.

Music 3 starts.

(sweetly) What "strange and mysterious" , Lady Dumsey?

LADY DUMSEY Oh, it's very hard to explain. It's all such a mystery.

SONG 3. "THE MYSTERY OF DUMSEY MEADOW" – Lady Dumsey, Mr Noble, Miss Featherstone, Children

THE STRANGEST THINGS ARE HAPPENING
I DON'T UNDERSTAND, IT'S SO CONFUSING
THE COWS AND SHEEP THEY FALL ASLEEP
THEN DANCE ROUND THE FIELD, IT'S SO BEMUSING
AND THE MILK TASTES AWFULLY FUNNY
GETTING WORSE
UN-NATURAL HISTORY
THE MYSTERY OF DUMSEY MEADOW

AND THOUGH I TRY TO CONTAIN IT
I CANNOT EXPLAIN IT
THE MYSTERY OF DUMSEY MEADOW

LADY D	MR NOBLE / MISS FEATHERSTONE	CHILDREN
AND THOUGH I TRY TO CONTAIN IT	AND THOUGH SHE TRIES TO CONTAIN IT	A MYSTERY
I CANNOT EXPLAIN IT	SHE CANNOT EXPLAIN IT	A REAL MYSTERY

SCENE ONE – ARRIVALS AND RIVALS

LADY D/MR NOBLE/MISS FEATHERSTONE/CHILDREN
THE MYSTERY OF DUMSEY MEADOW

LADY DUMSEY
THE WEIRDEST THINGS ARE TAKING PLACE
SO WATCH OUT, THE WARNING BELLS ARE RINGING
FARMER BILL, HE MUST BE ILL
HE CAN'T DO HIS WORK, HE'S ALWAYS SINGING
AND THE AIR SMELLS AWFULLY FUNNY
GETTING WORSE
IT'S QUITE A LIST, YOU SEE
THE MYSTERY OF DUMSEY MEADOW

I FIND I CAN'T UNDERSTAND IT
FOR NOBODY PLANNED IT
THE MYSTERY OF DUMSEY MEADOW

LADY D	**MR NOBLE/MISS FEATHERSTONE**	**CHILDREN**
I FIND I CAN'T UNDERSTAND IT	SHE FINDS SHE CAN'T UNDERSTAND IT	A MYSTERY

LADY D/MR NOBLE/MISS FEATHERSTONE   **CHILDREN**
FOR NOBODY PLANNED IT   A REAL MYSTERY

LADY D/MR NOBLE/MISS FEATHERSTONE/CHILDREN
THE MYSTERY OF DUMSEY MEADOW

LADY DUMSEY
NOW, EERIE THINGS HAVE COME TO PASS
THERE'S FEAR ALL AROUND, IT'S SO DEPRESSING
A SCARY CRY, THE RUMOURS FLY
THEY TALK OF A WITCH, IT'S SO DISTRESSING

I DON'T FIND THIS AWFULLY FUNNY
IT'S A CURSE
WISH IT WERE HISTORY
THE MYSTERY OF DUMSEY MEADOW

ALL
I'M SURE WE'LL ALL BE ENLIGHTENED

BUT NOW WE ARE FRIGHTENED
THE MYSTERY OF DUMSEY MEADOW

LADY D/MR NOBLE/MISS FEATHERSTONE   **CHILDREN**

I'M SURE WE'LL ALL BE ENLIGHTENED   A MYSTERY

BUT NOW WE ARE FRIGHTENED   A REAL MYSTERY

LADY D/MR NOBLE/MISS FEATHERSTONE
THE MYSTERY OF DUMSEY MEADOW

CHILDREN
THE MYSTERY

LADY D/MR NOBLE/MISS FEATHERSTONE
THE MYSTERY

CHILDREN
THE MYSTERY

LADY D/MR NOBLE/MISS FEATHERSTONE
THE MYSTERY

CHILDREN
THE MYSTERY

LADY D/MR NOBLE/MISS FEATHERSTONE
THE MYSTERY

ALL
THE MYSTERY

LADY D/MR NOBLE/MISS FEATHERSTONE
OF DUMSEY

ALL
MEADOW!

MISS FEATHERSTONE Well, you do seem to have a lot on your plate, Lady Dumsey.

ALEC All very interesting though. Crazy animals, a singing farmer, a strange smell—

SCENE ONE – ARRIVALS AND RIVALS   15

MR NOBLE Carter, please.

LADY DUMSEY The boy's right. There *is* a very unusual smell in the air these days. Sweet, strangely familiar and not altogether unpleasant.

MILLY And a witch! I can't wait to meet her, I've never met one before.

MISS FEATHERSTONE For goodness sake, Millicent. Can't you see Lady Dumsey is upset.

LADY DUMSEY So, I'm afraid I can't help you decide who stays, you'll have to sort it out yourselves – toss a coin or something. I'll come back at four o'clock – tea-time – to hear your decision and if you haven't decided by then you can *all* go home.

MISS FEATHERSTONE That doesn't give us long.

MR NOBLE How will we ever sort it out?

LADY DUMSEY That's up to you. I have a tiresome interview with the *Daily Herald* – someone's told the paper about our witch and they want to do a story. Can't imagine what I'll say. *(She starts to leave.)* I've got to visit the Vicar – his wife's not well, poor thing. Mystery illness. She makes lovely jam, you know. Oh and I must speak to that lazy, crazy farmer. No rest for the wicked, eh?

LADY DUMSEY *exits.*

GERALDINE Well, what a mess!

MISS FEATHERSTONE Geraldine Forster-Smythe, no battle was ever won with negative thoughts, you know that. We have to solve the problem swiftly, courageously and with great commitment.

MR NOBLE Well said, Miss Featherstone!

PORTER *(aside to the* **ST ALBERT'S CHILDREN***)* Nobby's such a wimp, he's already siding with the enemy.

MISS FEATHERSTONE What we need to devise is some sort of competition to determine which school stays. Do you agree, Mr Noble?

MR NOBLE A fine idea, Miss Featherstone. A fine idea. How about a physical contest?

CHILDREN (SA) *(nodding enthusiastically)* Yes!

MISS FEATHERSTONE Actually, I was thinking of something a little more...practical.

CHILDREN (SW) *(nodding enthusiastically)* Oh yes!

ALEC/MILLY Why don't we do both?

They look at each other and there is a moment of "connection".

SYLVIA Honestly, Milly, that's typical of you. Little Miss Clever Clogs.

PORTER *(mock politely)* Carter...shut up.

GERALDINE I think we should do both.

MISS FEATHERSTONE Good idea, Geraldine. As I said, we're not Head Girl for nothing, are we?

ALEC and MILLY look at each other and shrug their shoulders as if to say "what can you do?".

MR NOBLE Well, Jennings, as Head Boy of St Albert's, have you anything to say?

JENNINGS *(cockily)* Yes Sir, I have actually. *(thinking on his feet)* I think there should be a physical and a practical contest with, say, two challenges in each, and you and Miss Featherstone should decide what they are. But to make it fair, you should ask someone else to be the judge. A person from the village, perhaps?

MR NOBLE Well, well, Master Jennings. You are full of surprises.

JENNINGS *(imitating **MISS FEATHERSTONE**)* We aren't Head Boy for nothing, are we, Mr Noble?

The **ST ALBERT'S CHILDREN** *snigger and* **MR NOBLE** *gives him a withering look.*

MISS FEATHERSTONE Come along, Mr Noble, let's leave these "delightful" children to prepare themselves. We'll pop to the village to find our judges.

PERKINS I don't suppose they could have a competition for putting up tents?

MISS FEATHERSTONE And spoil all your fun, Perkins? That would never do.

__MISS FEATHERSTONE__ crosses to __MR NOBLE__ and they start to exit. They are stopped in their tracks by two __ELDERLY SISTERS__ who arrive on the scene and speak as if soothsayers.

MR NOBLE *(surprised by the sudden appearance of the* **SISTERS***)* Oh... Good morning, Ladies. Lovely day, isn't it?

DOROTHEA You mustn't stay here, there is too much to fear.

AGNES You must go away, it's too dangerous to stay.

DOROTHEA The meadow is haunted, the witch will come soon.

AGNES She's scary and creepy – tonight is full moon.

DOROTHEA So pick up your bags and be gone from this place.

AGNES A witch here in Dumsey,

DOROTHEA/AGNES It's such a disgrace!

They exit, tut-tutting.

__MR NOBLE__ and __MISS FEATHERSTONE__ look slightly taken aback.

CHILD (SW) Who on earth were they?

MISS FEATHERSTONE Pay no attention, they're just simple country folk.

CHILD (SW) Perhaps they're rehearsing for a play!

CHILD (SW) They were a bit scary.

GERALDINE Nonsense. St Winnie's children are never scared. Don't forget, "Fortune favours the bold".

MR NOBLE What a good saying, I must remember that.

MISS FEATHERSTONE Come along, Mr Noble, we must go. There isn't a moment to lose. Geraldine, you're in charge.

Music 3a starts as underscore.

The **TEACHERS** *exit.*

PORTER *(imitating* **MISS FEATHERSTONE***)* I say, Geraldine. You're in charge.

SYLVIA A competition – this is so exciting!

PORTER *(imitating* **SYLVIA***)* This is *so* exciting!

JENNINGS *(mocking)* How absolutely spiffing!

The **ST ALBERT'S CHILDREN** *are mimicking and mocking the* **ST WINIFRED'S CHILDREN***.*

ALEC *and* **MILLY** *stand at either side of the stage, not wanting to join in.*

SONG 3a. "HOW THRILLING!" – (Reprise #1) Children (not Alec/Milly)

CHILDREN (SW)
HOW THRILLING

CHILDREN (SA)
...HOW THRILLING

CHILDREN (SW)
HOW THRILLING

CHILDREN (SA)
...HOW THRILLING

SCENE ONE - ARRIVALS AND RIVALS

CHILDREN (SW)
IT REALLY IS SO ABSOLUTELY THRILLING

CHILDREN (SA)
... IT REALLY IS SO ABSOLUTELY THRILLING

CHILDREN (SW)
EXCITING!
INVITING!

CHILDREN (SA) *(spoken)*
ST ALBERT'S IS THE BEST, BEST, BEST
FAR BETTER THAN THE REST, REST, REST

CHILDREN (SW) *(sung)*
ST WINNIE'S!

CHILDREN (SA) *(spoken in time)* ...ST ALBERT'S!

CHILDREN (SW) *(sung)*
ST WINNIE'S!

CHILDREN (SA) *(spoken in time)* ...ST ALBERT'S!

CHILDREN (SW) *(sung)*
WE'LL SHOW YOU THAT YOU'RE SILLY, WEEDY NINNIES

CHILDREN (SA)
ST ALBERT'S IS THE BEST, BEST, BEST
FAR BETTER THAN THE REST, REST, REST

CHILDREN (SW)
WE'RE SUPER FIT, WE'LL MAKE THE GRADE
AND PROVE THAT WE ARE NOT AFRAID

JENNINGS *(spoken)* ST ALBERT'S SCHOOL IS GREAT, GREAT, GREAT

GERALDINE *(spoken)* COMPARED TO US, YOU'RE SECOND RATE

All the **CHILDREN** *start to exit.*

CHILDREN *(sung)*
IT REALLY, REALLY, REALLY IS
IT REALLY, REALLY, REALLY IS
IT REALLY IS SO ABSOLUTELY THRILLING!

The two schools exit in opposite directions as if to start practising for the competition in separate areas of the meadow. **PERKINS** *follows wearily.*

Scene Two – Meetings and Greetings
Somewhere on the Dumsey Estate

Music 3b.

A **HOODED WOMAN** *enters, crosses the stage. The mad, witch-like cackle is heard again (Effects 7). She exits.*

The **VICAR** *enters and inhales deeply as if for spiritual reassurance, then shows displeasure at the unusual smell he has inhaled.*

The **POLICEMAN, PC GREEN,** *enters on his way to Dumsey Meadow.*

PC GREEN Good morning, Vicar.

VICAR Good morning, PC Green. Everything tickety-boo?

PC GREEN Not really. I'm on my way to Dumsey Meadow, as it happens. There's been a disturbance.

VICAR Ah. That would explain the gunfire.

PC GREEN That was Lady Dumsey. She used her shotgun to calm down some overexcited schoolchildren.

VICAR Dear, dear. The youth of today. You know, PC Green, I was speaking to old Farmer Bill – he said he'd seen that witch again.

PC GREEN I wouldn't worry about what he says. He's gone a bit funny of late, always singing and imagining things. I need to see this witch for myself before I believe all the stories.

VICAR Well someone's told the papers and a journalist is coming here today to interview Lady Dumsey. *(to himself)* I hope she doesn't shoot *him*.

PC GREEN This is all out of hand, we don't want our village getting a reputation.

MR NOBLE *and* **MISS FEATHERSTONE** *enter.*

MISS FEATHERSTONE Good morning, gentlemen. I am Miss Featherstone and this is Mr Noble. We are teachers and were wondering if you could assist us in a rather important matter.

PC GREEN We'll certainly try, Miss, what seems to be the problem?

MR NOBLE Lady Dumsey has doublebooked the campsite.

PC GREEN *(to the* **VICAR***)* That's what I was telling you about.

MISS FEATHERSTONE And we need two judges for a competition this afternoon to determine which school stays in Dumsey Meadow.

PC GREEN That seems jolly fair – as long as you don't kill each other.

MR NOBLE There will be a physical and a practical contest.

MISS FEATHERSTONE Would you by chance be available and willing?

VICAR Happy to oblige – *(sadly)* anything to take my mind off my poor Mary.

PC GREEN I'll judge the physical contest if you like – I was rather athletic in my youth.

VICAR And I'll judge the practical one – I often helped my wife... *(sadly)* with her jam-making.

MISS FEATHERSTONE Thank you both very much.

PC GREEN In the meantime, I'll keep an eye on things in the meadow – we don't want any more trouble.

MISS FEATHERSTONE That's kind of you, Officer, but there's really no need.

PC GREEN All in the line of duty, Miss.

MISS FEATHERSTONE Very well. We will see you there later. The contest will start at three o'clock.

VICAR I'll keep you company, PC Green. *(doffing his hat)* Miss Featherstone, Mr Noble, good morning to you.

The **VICAR** *and the* **POLICEMAN** *exit.*

MR NOBLE What jolly decent fellows.

MISS FEATHERSTONE Indeed, Mr Noble. I'm glad that's sorted.

MR NOBLE *and* **MISS FEATHERSTONE** *go to exit but are stopped in their tracks by the entrance of the* **ELDERLY SISTERS**.

DOROTHEA We told you all to go away,

We said it wasn't safe to stay.

AGNES The children will get such a fright,

When the witch appears at dead of night.

DOROTHEA Go now, before it's much too late.

AGNES Before the witch has sealed your fate.

DOROTHEA We've warned you twice, now off you go.

AGNES You mustn't stay—

DOROTHEA/AGNES And we should know!

They chuckle conspiratorially, causing their aged backs to spasm, which they clutch in pain before exiting. **PERKINS** *trudges on very slowly, weighed down with yet more camping equipment.*

MR NOBLE Well, Miss Featherstone. That's the second time they've warned us about the witch. I think there might be something in it.

MISS FEATHERSTONE I think they're crackers.

MR NOBLE But it solves our problem.

MISS FEATHERSTONE *(curtly)* Hmm. Does it now?

MR NOBLE Oh yes, St Albert's should stay. The boys study self-defence and wouldn't be frightened even if a witch *were* to appear in the night.

MISS FEATHERSTONE Well, we train *our* pupils to be self-reliant and quick-thinking – they are fiendish at hockey and are able to knock up a Victoria sponge cake at very short notice. Perkins knows what Winnies are made of, don't you Perkins?

PERKINS *(exiting)* Give up now, Sir, that's my advice.

PERKINS exits.

MR NOBLE Well then, it will be a fair fight, Miss Featherstone.

MISS FEATHERSTONE Indeed, Mr Noble. See you on the battlefield at three o'clock sharp.

BOTH *(nodding emphatically)* Agreed!

They exit.

Music 3c.

Scene Three – Witches and Warnings
Dumsey Meadow

The ST ALBERT'S CHILDREN *are practising their physical skills.*

ALEC *(practising weight-lifting with a branch)* If there's a weight-lifting competition, I'd really like to do it.

CHILD (SA) Don't be stupid, Alec, you're too weedy. I'm the strongest, I should do it.

CHILD (SA) No you're not, I'm easily stronger than you.

PORTER We all know I'm the St Albert's muscle man – there's no one stronger than me.

ALEC I think you should stop arguing and start practising – that would be more useful.

JENNINGS Did someone speak? *(to* ALEC*)* Oh, it's you, Carter. Couldn't see you there under that twig.

PORTER Weedy *and* bossy. Not good qualities for an Albert's boy, are they?

ALEC I shall choose to ignore these comments – I'd rather be small and brainy, than big and stupid.

JENNINGS Watch it, weedy!

PORTER He's trying to live up to his name – Smart Alec.

ALEC As it happens, I'm formulating a theory about all the strange things going on here in Dumsey Meadow. But you wouldn't be interested.

JENNINGS Try me.

ALEC Well, firstly, I think there's a connection between the unusual smell and the peculiar behaviour of the farmer and his animals.

CHILD (SA) Honestly, you've got a weird brain, Carter.

ALEC Thank you. And secondly, all this talk of witches is complete nonsense because they don't exist, except in fairy tales.

CHILD (SA) Of course they do. Why do you think everyone's so scared?

ALEC They're only scared because someone wants them to be scared. It's basic psychology.

PORTER Have you swallowed a dictionary?

He walks over to **ALEC** *threateningly.*

Well, Carter. *(raising his fist as if to punch* **ALEC**) Maybe you should swallow this.

JENNINGS *(looking offstage)* Crikey, Porter, look! It's the Old Bill!

They hurriedly resume their training.

PC GREEN *and the* **VICAR** *enter.*

PC GREEN 'Allo, 'allo, 'allo, what's going on 'ere then?

PORTER Nothing, Officer.

VICAR Good morning, children, I see you're in training for the competition.

JENNINGS Yes, Sir. We've got to beat the other school so that we can stay here for our camping trip.

PORTER *(pointing offstage to "another part of the meadow")* They're over there, doing needlework and knitting. They don't stand a chance against us.

PC GREEN Don't be so sure, young lad – a knitting needle in the wrong hands could prove fatal. *(He prods* **PORTER** *with his truncheon.)* I'll go and keep an eye on them. Vicar, you stay here.

He exits.

SCENE THREE – WITCHES AND WARNINGS

VICAR I must say, you children sound awfully confident, but we shall see. "The proof of the pudding", as they say!

ALEC Talking of proof, what's the truth about this witch everyone's scared of?

CHILD (SA) Yes, does she really exist?

VICAR Witches don't exist and they never have.

ALEC That's just what I told them.

VICAR But Dumsey has a story about a woman they *called* a witch that goes back three hundred years.

CHILD (SA) What's the story?

VICAR In 1638, a local woman, Old Nancy Fairweather, was blamed for the failed apple harvest.

ALEC *(curiously)* A failed apple harvest?

VICAR That's right – the apples mysteriously rotted on the trees.

ALEC And now, three hundred years later, it's happened again.

CHILD (SA) What became of Old Nancy Fairweather?

VICAR She was burnt at the stake right here in Dumsey Meadow.

The **CHILDREN** *gasp.*

JENNINGS *(trying to scare the other* **CHILDREN***)* Maybe she's come back to haunt the meadow.

Music 4 starts as underscore.

PORTER *(joining* **JENNINGS** *in trying to scare the others)* Oooooooooooh! A ghost! The witch's ghost!

VICAR/ALEC Nonsense!

During the introduction to the song, the **CHILDREN** *start pretending to be ghosts and witches etc.*

THE MYSTERY OF DUMSEY MEADOW

SONG 4. "WITCHES ARE BEWITCHING" – Vicar, Alec, Jennings, Porter, Children (SA)

VICAR

>IN OLDEN DAYS A WITCH, THEY SAID
>WAS SOMEONE WHO HAD DARED
>TO THREATEN WITH THE EVIL-EYE
>AND MAKE THE PEOPLE SCARED
>A WITCH POSSESSED GREAT PSYCHIC SKILLS
>OR SO THE LEGENDS CLAIM
>BUT REALLY IT WAS JUST A SILLY GAME
>
>ALL WITCHERY IS MAKE BELIEVE
>DESIGNED TO THRILL AND SCARE
>THEY WANT YOU TO BE FRIGHTENED, SO BEWARE!

CHILDREN (SA)

>WITCHES ARE BEWITCHING SO BEWARE
>THEIR CHARMS AND MAGIC POTIONS FILL THE AIR
>WITH RITUALS AND RHYMES INGENIOUS
>THEY'LL CONJURE UP A SPELL THAT'S DANGEROUS
>AND USE A BROOMSTICK RATHER THAN THE BUS

ALEC You should listen to what the Vicar says. Everything about witches is just made up.

VICAR

>POOR ANNE BOLEYN WAS CALLED A WITCH
>THROUGH NO FAULT OF HER OWN
>SIX FINGERS ON HER FAIR LEFT HAND
>MEANT "GET HER OFF THE THRONE!"
>WHEN HENRY SAW THE TINY MOLE
>UPON HER DAINTY NECK
>HER HEAD WAS WELL AND TRULY FOR THE DECK

GROUP 1 (SA)

>RAPUNZEL WASN'T HAPPY WHEN
>THE NASTY WICKED CRONE
>LOCKED HER UP INSIDE THE TOW'R
>AND LEFT HER ON HER OWN

SCENE THREE – WITCHES AND WARNINGS

GROUP 2 (SA)
SNOW WHITE WAS TEMPTED BY A WITCH
WHOSE ROSY APPLE RED
CONTAINED A SPELL THAT LEFT HER NEARLY DEAD

VICAR
BUT DON'T BELIEVE IN ALL YOU READ

ALEC
THE VICAR SPEAKS THE TRUTH

CHILDREN (SA)
THE WITCHING HOUR APPROACHES, FIE! FORESOOTH!

CHILDREN (SA)
WITCHES ARE BEWITCHING SO BEWARE
THEIR CHARMS AND MAGIC POTIONS FILL THE AIR
THEY BUBBLE UP A CAULDRON JUST FOR FUN
AND THROW IN NAUGHTY CHILDREN ONE BY ONE
THEN EAT THEM FOR THEIR SUPPER IN A BUN!

ALEC You're not listening, are you? There's no such thing as a witch.

VICAR
THE WITCHY FOLK WERE TORTURED FOR
A CRIME THEY KNEW WAS FAKE
THEY'D FORCE THEM TO CONFESS AND THEN
THEY'D BURN THEM AT THE STAKE

PORTER
THE DUMSEY WITCH WAS EVIL SO HER FATE WAS JUST THE SAME

JENNINGS
AND NOW SHE'S BACK TO CLEAR HER WICKED NAME

VICAR
BUT DON'T BELIEVE IN ALL YOU SEE

ALEC
IT SIMPLY ISN'T TRUE

VICAR/ALEC
IT'S REALLY NOT A CLEVER THING TO DO

CHILDREN (SA)
WITCHES ARE BEWITCHING SO BEWARE

VICAR/ALEC
THAT'S QUITE ENOUGH OF THAT

CHILDREN (SA)
THEIR CHARMS AND MAGIC POTIONS FILL THE AIR

VICAR/ALEC
NOW STOP YOUR FOOLISH CHAT

CHILDREN (SA)
WITH EYE OF TOAD AND CARCASS OF A RAT

VICAR/ALEC
IT SIMPLY ISN'T TRUE

CHILDREN (SA)
WITH WARTY FACE AND POINTY, BIG, BLACK HAT

VICAR/ALEC
AND THAT'S ALL NONSENSE TOO

CHILDREN (SA)
THEY'LL TURN YOU INTO STONE AND THAT IS THAT!

VICAR
SO DON'T BELIEVE IN ALL YOU HEAR
JUST KEEP A LEVEL HEAD
THE DUMSEY WITCH IS WELL AND TRULY DEAD

CHILDREN (SA)
WITH BATS AND FAT COCKROACHES

VICAR/ALEC
THE FANTASY ENCROACHES

CHILDREN (SA)
THE WITCHING HOUR APPROACHES

ALL
SO BEWARE!

SCENE THREE – WITCHES AND WARNINGS

We hear the manic laugh again (Effects 8) and the **HOODED WOMAN** *appears briefly then vanishes. The* **CHILDREN** *see her and they are all, apart from* **ALEC**, *very frightened.*

VICAR *(shouting above the din the* **CHILDREN** *are making)* Children, children. There's no need to panic. There's nothing to be frightened of.

The **VICAR** *and the* **CHILDREN** *exit.* **ALEC** *remains behind.*

ALEC No need to panic, Alec. I'm sure there's a logical, scientific explanation for all of this.

We hear the **FARMER** *offstage singing* **"THE GLADNESS OF THE MAY"** *(unaccompanied).* **ALEC** *"hides". The* **FARMER** *enters and crosses the stage, still singing, then exits.*

The singing farmer! I'll follow him.

ALEC *goes to exit.*

The **JOURNALIST** *enters from the opposite side.*

JOURNALIST *(calling after* **ALEC**) I say, young man.

ALEC *stops and turns round.*

Harry Fleet, *Daily Herald*. What's all the commotion about? Is it the witch?

ALEC *(pointing to where the* **ST WINIFRED'S CHILDREN** *are coming on)* Ask them.

He runs off in pursuit of the **FARMER**.

Scene Four – Law and Order
Dumsey Meadow

The **ST WINIFRED'S CHILDREN** *enter, followed by the* **POLICEMAN**, *in response to all the commotion. The girls are brandishing hockey and lacrosse sticks, tennis and badminton racquets etc.*

The **JOURNALIST** *starts taking photographs and firing questions at the* **CHILDREN**.

JOURNALIST Harry Fleet, *Daily Herald*. What do you know about the witch? Have you seen the witch? What does she look like? Are you scared?

SYLVIA St Winnie's pupils are *never* scared.

PC GREEN *(He blows his whistle and ushers them out of the way.)* No need for concern, everyone. Stand well back now, stand well back. Clear the way please.

JOURNALIST *(continuing to ask the* **CHILDREN** *questions)* What's going on? Was the witch here? Did you see her? Does she exist?

CHILD (SW) Of course she does, she was here just now.

CHILD (SW) We're going to capture her and torture her.

CHILD (SW) It'll be such fun.

PC GREEN Pardon me, Sir, but you must refrain from asking questions. I assume you are here from the paper to interview Lady Dumsey?

JOURNALIST That's right, Harry Fleet, *Daily Herald* – I'm meeting Lady Dumsey in the village at lunchtime. I heard a commotion and came to see what was going on. *(asking the* **CHILDREN***)* So, children, tell me about this witch.

MILLY We mustn't jump to conclusions. The person who people think is a witch, may not be all that she seems.

SCENE FOUR – LAW AND ORDER

GERALDINE Don't be silly, Milly. Of course she's a witch.

SYLVIA And we'll make her sorry for trying to scare us. Isn't that right, everyone?

CHILDREN (SW) Hear, hear!

PC GREEN I'm afraid I'm going to have to ask you to move along please, Sir. *(pointing in the relevant direction)* The village is that way.

JOURNALIST Very well. Thank you, Officer. I'll get the full story from Lady Dumsey later. *(aside, going to exit)* Now, where's that witch?

The **JOURNALIST** *exits, camera at the ready. With great curiosity* **MILLY** *goes to follow him, but stops in her tracks as* **PC GREEN** *speaks.*

PC GREEN Now then, children. A word of warning. Don't go talking to that journalist, or anyone else, about what's going on here in Dumsey. Nobody knows for sure and we don't want rumours flying around that might do more harm than good.

GERALDINE We're only trying to help, Sir.

SYLVIA Maybe we'll catch the witch for you.

Music 5 starts as underscore.

PC GREEN It's good of you to offer, but this kind of thing should be left to us professionals. Fighting crime and solving mysteries is for experts only.

Throughout the song, **MILLY** *sits to one side, making notes in her notebook.*

SONG 5. *"BOBBY ON THE BEAT"* – PC Green, Geraldine, Sylvia, Children (SW) (not Milly)

I AM PROUD TO BELONG TO THE FORCE THAT FIGHTS THE FOE
AND I ALWAYS DO MY BEST TO SOLVE THE CRIME

I GET A LOT OF PLEASURE
WHEN I CAPTURE AT MY LEISURE
A BADDIE, AND I MAKE HIM SERVE HIS TIME

UPHOLDING LAW AND ORDER IS THE THING I DO THE BEST
AND YOU SHOULDN'T UNDERESTIMATE THE TASK
I'M FULL OF USEFUL KNOWLEDGE
'CAUSE I STUDIED HARD AT COLLEGE
SO IF YOU WANT TO KNOW THE TIME, JUST ASK

'ALLO, 'ALLO, 'ALLO, I'M A BOBBY ON THE BEAT
I'M ALWAYS MOST POLITE
TO EVERYONE I MEET
IT'S THE DUTY OF A BOBBY
TO MAKE SURE HE DOES HIS JOBBY
AND TO KEEP CRIME WELL AND TRULY OFF THE STREET

CHILDREN (SW)
WE WOULD LIKE TO GET INVOLVED
AND WE'RE VERY KEEN TO HELP
THE WICKED WITCH WOULD NEVER STAND A CHANCE
WE COULD APPREHEND THIS PEST
WITH A CITIZEN'S ARREST
WE'RE EAGER AND WE'RE READY TO ADVANCE

PC GREEN
NOW HANG ON JUST A MINUTE AND PLEASE LISTEN TO THE PRO
YOU CAN'T RUSH IN WHERE ANGELS FEAR TO TREAD
I DO MY FITNESS TRAINING
IN THE SUN AND WHEN IT'S RAINING
SO LEAVE IT TO THE EXPERT LIKE I SAID

ALL
'ALLO, 'ALLO, 'ALLO, I'M /HE'S A BOBBY ON THE BEAT
I'M /HE'S ALWAYS MOST POLITE
TO EVERYONE I /HE MEET/S
IT'S THE DUTY OF A BOBBY
TO MAKE SURE HE DOES HIS JOBBY
AND TO KEEP CRIME WELL AND TRULY OFF THE STREET

SCENE FOUR – LAW AND ORDER

GERALDINE
> WE WILL USE OUR JOLLY HOCKEY STICKS
> TO MAKE THE WITCH CONFESS

PC GREEN
> NOW STEADY ON
> THAT'S SIMPLY NOT FAIR PLAY

SYLVIA
> WE WILL MAKE HER QUAKE AND QUIVER
> 'TILL THE TRUTH SHE WILL DELIVER

PC GREEN
> FIGHTING CRIME WITH CRIME
> WILL NEVER PAY
>
> THE MOST SUCCESSFUL POLICEMEN ARE ALL EXTREMELY BRIGHT
> AND THEY'RE AGILE AND THEY'D NEVER BE UNCOUTH
> THEY ALWAYS STOP FOR LUNCHEON
> BEFORE SHINING UP THEIR TRUNCHEON
> THEY KNOW THE WAY TO BE A SUPER SLEUTH

CHILDREN (SW)
> WE'RE STEALTHY AND WE'RE WEALTHY
> AND OUR HEARTS WOULD FILL WITH PRIDE
> TO THINK THAT WE COULD SERVE WITHIN THE FORCE
> WE'RE ALWAYS NEAT AND PUNCTUAL
> WITH WEAPONS THAT ARE FUNCTIONAL
> WE'RE COVERED FOR INSURANCE CLAIMS OF COURSE!

ALL
> 'ALLO, 'ALLO, 'ALLO, I'M/HE'S A BOBBY ON THE BEAT
> I'M /HE'S ALWAYS MOST POLITE
> TO EVERYONE I /HE MEET/S

CHILDREN (SW)
> THIS REALLY IS A THRILL!

PC GREEN
> YOU MUST LEAVE IT TO THE BILL

CHILDREN (SW)
>DETECTIVE WORK IS BRILL!

PC GREEN
>I'M THE ONE WITH ALL THE SKILL, FOR I'M A BOBBY

CHILDREN (SW)
>HE'S A BOBBY

PC GREEN
>I'M A BOBBY

CHILDREN (SW)
>WITH A JOBBY

ALL
>I'M / HE'S A BOBBY, BOBBY, BOBBY, BOBBY, BOBBY, BOBBY, BOBBY ON THE BEAT
>BOBBY ON THE BEAT
>BOBBY ON THE BEAT
>BOBBY ON THE—

CHILD (SW) 'Allo, 'Allo, 'Allo, what's going on 'ere then?

ALL
>BEAT!

PC GREEN I shall be back at three o'clock to help judge your competition – I suggest you focus on that. And don't go torturing any witches!

He exits.

GERALDINE He's right, everyone. Come on, let's get practising. We've got to win this competition.

SYLVIA *(wickedly)* Then we can capture the witch – and torture her.

GERALDINE Alright, St Winnie's – twenty star jumps. Ready? Out, in, out, in…

They start to do star jumps, **MILLY** *gets up to join in.*

SYLVIA You won't be able to compete, Milly. You're too little.

SCENE FOUR – LAW AND ORDER

GERALDINE Too little to be here, if you ask me.

MILLY I may be little, but I'm going to show you all that bigger isn't better.

The other **CHILDREN** *ignore* **MILLY**'s *comment and continue with their star jumps.*

(*proudly*) I'm not afraid and I'm going to solve the mystery of the witch of Dumsey Meadow! (*thoughtfully*) Maybe I'll find some clues in the village.

She exits.

GERALDINE Ignore her, she's just showing off. Right, St Winnie's, three times round the meadow. Off we go, left, right, left, right, left, right.

Music 5a.

The **ST WINIFRED'S CHILDREN** *complete a circuit then exit, with* **GERALDINE** *shouting her commands until they are all offstage.*

Scene Five – Reason and Rhyme
Somewhere on the Dumsey Estate

LADY DUMSEY *and the* **VICAR** *enter from opposite sides and meet.*

LADY DUMSEY Good morning, Vicar. *(sympathetically)* How are you today?

VICAR Oh, Virginia, the world is going mad. The Dumsey witch stories are causing widespread panic. What are we to do?

MILLY *enters, sees the* **VICAR** *and* **LADY DUMSEY** *and seizes the opportunity to gather some valuable information. She "hides" within earshot and listens and observes without being seen. During the conversation, she makes notes in her notebook.*

LADY DUMSEY You can't stop village gossip, Vicar. People will always talk.

VICAR Witches, ghosts, history repeating itself, everyone's in a panic – last Sunday the church was full to bursting. It's a job, you know, especially with my wife being away.

LADY DUMSEY Is there any news of her?

VICAR Yes, a telegram arrived this morning. The doctors at the Bracklesea clinic think it will be some time before she's better. Her illness is quite a mystery – one day fine, the next she was feeling terribly out of sorts.

LADY DUMSEY Poor Mary – what a shock and such a pity. She was greatly missed in the recent Dumsey Players production at the village hall. Let's hope she's back in time for the pantomime, she's a fine actress.

VICAR How kind of you to say so.

LADY DUMSEY And no one makes better jam than Mary – I've almost run out.

SCENE FIVE – REASON AND RHYME

VICAR If you'll excuse me, Virginia, I must be off now. I'm helping judge the competition to decide who camps in your meadow.

LADY DUMSEY That blasted double booking – how jolly tiresome! I shall be there at four o'clock, and I hope for their sake that it's all sorted out.

VICAR Good day, Virginia.

*The **VICAR** doffs his hat at **LADY DUMSEY** and exits.*

MILLY *(aside, from her hiding place)* Golly, how interesting! I shall have to make some enquiries.

She accidentally drops her pencil.

LADY DUMSEY *(hearing the noise and noticing **MILLY**, she is taken aback)* What are you doing, child?

MILLY I'm...um...I'm...

LADY DUMSEY Well?

MILLY I'm... *(suddenly thinking of an explanation)* doing a history project.

LADY DUMSEY Well, you shouldn't be wandering around on your own, it's not safe. You should be with your school.

MILLY Of course, Lady Dumsey. I'll do my project later.

LADY DUMSEY Now run along or you'll miss the competition.

MILLY *exits.*

***LADY DUMSEY** goes to leave, then hears the **FARMER** singing "THE GLADNESS OF THE MAY" (unaccompanied). She stops and winces at the horrendous sound.*

*The **FARMER** enters, still in a jolly mood, followed by **ALEC** who "hides". During the dialogue, **ALEC** listens and observes without being seen.*

Ah, Farmer Bill. I need to speak to you on a serious matter.

FARMER BILL *continues to sing and gently sway.*

Farmer Bill, would you please stop singing and swaying, and listen to me.

FARMER BILL I'm sorry, Lady D, but I'm afraid I can't help it. I can't stop singing. I don't know why, but I feel so happy that I just want to *(singing these words)* sing and dance!

LADY DUMSEY Well, it's all jolly tiresome, Farmer Bill, when you've got work to do. And what does your wife think about it?

FARMER BILL Doesn't bother her, Ma'am. Mind you, she's not herself these days. She keeps *(mysteriously)* ..."disappearing" and when she comes home she's usually laughing like a madwoman... *(matter-of-factly)* and then she falls asleep.

LADY DUMSEY How very... "mysterious".

FARMER BILL I think it's funny. And the sheep and cows think so too. *(He "bahs" like a singing sheep and "moos" like a singing cow.)*

LADY DUMSEY This has got to stop. Can't you see how much work there is to do?

SONG 6. "THINGS TO DO" – Lady Dumsey, Farmer Bill

FARMER BILL, I'M WORRIED
SO I FEEL I HAVE TO ASK
WHY OF LATE YOU'RE ALWAYS SINGING
YET NEGLECTFUL OF YOUR TASK
THERE ARE MANY MORE IMPORTANT THINGS TO DO

She consults her list.

THERE'S PLOUGHING AND PRUNING AND SEED THAT NEEDS SOWING
THERE'S CUTTING AND CLEARING AND GRASS THAT NEEDS MOWING
THERE'S FIELDS THAT NEED HEDGING

AND PONDS THAT NEED DREDGING
THERE'S PICKING AND FEEDING AND SPRAYING AND WEEDING AND—

FARMER BILL
AND SINGING!

LADY DUMSEY And singing?!

FARMER BILL
AND SINGING!

LADY DUMSEY This is ridiculous!

FARMER
I LIKE TO SING A JOLLY SONG
I WANT THE WORLD TO SING ALONG
AND WHEN I SING, SUCH JOY I BRING
FOR SINGING IS A HAPPY THING

LADY DUMSEY Well you're certainly not bringing me any joy. It's so unlike you to be happy, I'm beginning to have my suspicions.
(sung)
YOU'RE NORMALLY SO GRUMPY
NOW YOU HUM A MERRY TUNE
PERHAPS YOU'RE ON THE BOTTLE
EVERY MORNING, NIGHT AND NOON?
THINK OF ALL THE MANY THINGS YOU HAVE TO DO

THERE'S MULCHING AND MILKING AND LAMBS THAT NEED REARING
THERE'S PLANTING AND REAPING AND SHEEP THAT NEED SHEARING
THERE'S COWS THAT NEED BEDDING
AND MUCK THAT NEEDS SPREADING
THERE'S BRANDING AND CLIPPING AND TRIMMING AND DIPPING AND—

FARMER BILL
AND DANCING!

LADY DUMSEY And dancing?!

FARMER BILL
> AND DANCING!

LADY DUMSEY This is preposterous!

FARMER BILL
> I LIKE TO MOVE, I WANT TO DANCE
> THE SWAYING PUTS ME IN A TRANCE
> OH I'M THE KING, THE KING OF SWING
> AND LADY D, TO YOU I'LL CLING

They dance.

LADY DUMSEY *(pushing him away)* That's quite enough of that!

FARMER BILL
> THERE'S NOTHING I CAN DO ABOUT IT
> I DON'T KNOW HOW TO LIVE WITHOUT IT
> I NEED TO SING
> SING AND DANCE THE WHOLE DAY THROUGH

LADY DUMSEY
> YOUR BEHAVIOUR IS APPALLING
> THERE ARE MANY MORE IMPORTANT THINGS TO DO

They sing simultaneously...

FARMER BILL
> {I LIKE TO SING A JOLLY SONG
> {I WANT THE WORLD TO SING ALONG
> {AND WHEN I SING, SUCH JOY I BRING
> {FOR SINGING IS A HAPPY THING

LADY DUMSEY
> {THERE'S PLOUGHING AND PRUNING AND SEED THAT NEEDS SOWING
> {THERE'S CUTTING AND CLEARING AND GRASS THAT NEEDS MOWING
> {THERE'S FIELDS THAT NEED HEDGING
> {AND PONDS THAT NEED DREDGING
> {BUT THERE ARE MANY THINGS TO DO

SCENE FIVE – REASON AND RHYME

FARMER BILL
{I LIKE TO MOVE, I WANT TO DANCE
{THE SWAYING PUTS ME IN A TRANCE
{OH I'M THE KING, THE KING OF SWING

LADY DUMSEY
{THERE'S MULCHING AND MILKING AND LAMBS THAT NEED REARING
{THERE'S PLANTING AND REAPING AND SHEEP THAT NEED SHEARING
{THERE'S COWS THAT NEED BEDDING
{AND MUCK THAT NEEDS SPREADING

FARMER BILL
I'M DANCING

LADY DUMSEY
STOP PRANCING!

FARMER BILL
AND SWAYING

LADY DUMSEY *(spoken in time)* I'M PAYING!

FARMER BILL *(sung)*
AND SINGING

LADY DUMSEY
THERE ARE MANY THINGS TO DO

FARMER BILL
FA LA LA LA LA LA LA LA!

LADY DUMSEY Farmer Bill, I must say that following such an "unusual" display of terpsichorean talent, I can only assume you have been drinking.

FARMER BILL Oh no, Lady D, I'm completely tea-total.

LADY DUMSEY *(jokingly)* Well, you obviously aren't making your tea with water then!

FARMER BILL *(an afterthought)* Oh, there is the communion wine on a Sunday of course, but that—

LADY DUMSEY Yes, I've noticed you in church recently. That's unusual too, if I may say so.

FARMER BILL Well, I don't like all this talk of witches – it's scary. And the church is a grand place for a sing-song. *(singing)* WE PLOUGH THE FIELDS AND SCATTER—

LADY DUMSEY *(shrieking)* Stop!! I wish you *would* plough the fields and scatter! Now, have you disposed of all those rotten apples yet?

FARMER BILL Yes, Ma'am. I've made a nice big heap of them at the bottom of the orchard. They're rotting down nicely for next year's compost.

LADY DUMSEY Well, that's something. Now get on with your other jobs please. And do stop singing, it's costing me money.

FARMER BILL *(doffing his cap at* **LADY DUMSEY***)* Lady D.

He starts to exit, singing.

WE PLOUGH THE FIELDS AND...

Oops, sorry m'Lady.

He exits.

ALEC *comes out of hiding and follows the* **FARMER** *off.*

As **LADY DUMSEY** *turns to leave, the* **JOURNALIST** *enters, followed by* **MILLY***, who listens and observes without being seen as she makes notes in her book.*

JOURNALIST Excuse me, I'm looking for Lady Dumsey. Do you know her?

LADY DUMSEY I *am* her!

JOURNALIST Marvellous. Harry Fleet, *Daily Herald*. I'm here to do your interview about the witch.

LADY DUMSEY Ah yes. Good. I was wondering where you might have got to. *(quietly)* We did agree seventy-five pounds, didn't we? Do you have the cash with you?

SCENE FIVE – REASON AND RHYME

JOURNALIST I do indeed and I will be happy to pass it on to you once the interview is "in the bag" as we say in the business.

LADY DUMSEY Jolly good. I thought we could find a quiet corner at the Dumsey Arms.

JOURNALIST That sounds grand. I'm in your hands, Lady Dumsey.

They exit.

MILLY *emerges from her hiding place.*

MILLY Golly, how interesting! *(referring to her notes)* Now then, let's see what I've got so far. First there was that, then that...and that...oh yes, that was important...

She makes some more notes.

Music 6a.

The **HOODED WOMAN** *enters behind* **MILLY** *and walks slowly up to her in a menacing manner.* **MILLY** *is unaware of this, as she is facing downstage.*

If only I could meet the witch. That would be really fascinating... I'd just like to ask her a few questions...

As the **HOODED WOMAN** *reaches* **MILLY**, *the music reaches a climax and she raises both arms in a threatening gesture.* **MILLY** *is still unaware.*

I don't think I'd be scared...

The action freezes.

If an interval is required, this is where it would be. Act Two would begin with the above tableau, as if no time had passed. Music 6a would pick up at its loudest point.

DOROTHEA *(loudly, as she enters)* Beware! Beware!

MILLY *jumps when she hears this and turns round. She sees the* **HOODED WOMAN** *and is surprised and excited. The* **HOODED WOMAN** *scuttles off in the same direction as* **LADY DUMSEY** *and the* **JOURNALIST.**

DOROTHEA We *told* you all to go away, We said it wasn't safe to stay.

MILLY You made me jump!

DOROTHEA The witch was here, yet you showed no fear.

MILLY I know, wasn't it exciting? *(crossly)* And you scared her off.

DOROTHEA You should beware, you must take care.

MILLY *(suspiciously)* Hmmn...there were two of you before. Where's your friend?

DOROTHEA My *sister*, Agnes, will join me soon,

She's... *(struggling to think where her sister is)*

Er...she's...lost her favourite silver spoon.

MILLY Oh. I hope she finds it. Why do you always talk in rhyme?

DOROTHEA You speak as though it were a crime.

MILLY I've never met anyone who talks like you.

DOROTHEA Your manner, girl, is rude, but typical. The young these days are so... *(struggling to find a rhyme)* ...despicable.

MILLY Isn't it boring speaking in rhyme the whole time? *(Realising she has just rhymed, she gasps.)* Oh no, it's catching!

AGNES, *the other* **ELDERLY SISTER**, *enters from the same place as the* **HOODED WOMAN** *exited. She is slightly flustered and is adjusting an item of clothing.*

DOROTHEA Ah sister, dear, you're here at last.

AGNES Surprising how the time has passed.

MILLY *(innocently)* Did you find your spoon?

SCENE FIVE - REASON AND RHYME

DOROTHEA *(quickly jumping in)* This child has an enquiring mind. She's different from the usual kind. She asked me why we speak this way.

AGNES And did you tell? Or won't we say?

MILLY What fun, you do it every time.

DOROTHEA/AGNES Of course, we are the Sisters of Rhyme!

DOROTHEA and AGNES look at each other and cackle.

SONG 7. "SISTERS OF RHYME" - Milly, Dorothea, Agnes

MILLY *(spoken)* YOUR RHMING GAME IS QUITE ABSURD.

DOROTHEA *(spoken)* YET WE ALWAYS FIND A MATCHING WORD.

The SISTERS giggle gleefully at their ability.

MILLY *(under her breath)* Right, let's see how good they really are.

(spoken) I THINK I'LL GO AND WRITE AN "ARTICLE".

AGNES *(spoken)* WHAT NONSENSE, THAT WOULD BE SO... "FARCICAL".

MILLY *(spoken)* YOUR TALENTS SHOULD BE IN A... "CHRONICLE".

DOROTHEA *(spoken)* THAT I COULD LOOK AT THROUGH MY... "MONOCLE".

MILLY *(sung)*
  I THINK THERE'S NOTHING TO IT

DOROTHEA/AGNES *(sung)*
  BUT YOU COULD NEVER DO IT

DOROTHEA Ready, sister?

AGNES After you, dear.

During this chorus of the song, DOROTHEA and AGNES take great pleasure in their ability to rhyme, congratulating each other with positive smiles and winks.

DOROTHEA
YOU TAKE A GATE AND SWING IT 'TIL IT'S OPEN

AGNES
YOU TAKE A PLATE AND SMASH IT 'TIL IT'S BROKEN

DOROTHEA
YOU TAKE A CAT THAT IS A LITTLE CURIOUS

AGNES
YOU WEAR A HAT THAT MAKES THE VICAR FURIOUS

DOROTHEA
YOU TELL A TALE WHICH LASTS AD INFINITUM

AGNES
YOU EAT A SNAIL AND SAY IT'S JUST TO SPITE 'EM

DOROTHEA/AGNES
WE CAN DO IT EVERY TIME
WE'RE THE FAMOUS SISTERS OF RHYME!

Music 7 continues as underscore.

MILLY You still haven't told me why you do it.

DOROTHEA The answer lies within this book.

She takes a large, dusty book out of her bag.

AGNES Take it child and have a look.

MILLY *takes the book and reads the title.*

MILLY The History of Fairy Tales.

AGNES It cost three shillings, bought in Wales!

DOROTHEA
THIS BOOK HAS ALL THE SCARY TALES

AGNES
THE POWER OF THEM NEVER FAILS

DOROTHEA
YOUNG CHILDREN LEARN TO BE AFRAID

SCENE FIVE – REASON AND RHYME

AGNES
OF WICKED WITCH IN WOODED GLADE

DOROTHEA
AND WORDS WHICH RHYME CAN MAKE THEM SCARED

AGNES
TO WARN THEM THEY SHOULD BE PREPARED

DOROTHEA/AGNES
OUR RHYMES ARE ALWAYS CLEVER

MILLY
BET I COULD DO IT

DOROTHEA/AGNES
NEVER!

DOROTHEA Well, sister, shall we let her try?

AGNES Let's make it hard and then she'll cry.

They laugh conspiratorially.

MILLY Ready when you are.

During the rest of the song, **DOROTHEA** *and* **AGNES** *become increasingly irritated by* **MILLY**'s *skill at rhyming and begin to "huff and puff" with annoyance.* **MILLY** *becomes increasingly excited and pleased with her ability to rhyme.*

DOROTHEA
YOU HAVE AN ACHE BECAUSE YOU'VE BEEN SO BUSY

MILLY
YOU BURN A CAKE AND END UP IN A TIZZY

AGNES
YOU TAKE A FLIGHT TO CAIRO IN AN AEROPLANE

MILLY
YOU FLY A KITE THAT'S MADE OF YELLOW CELLOPHANE

DOROTHEA
YOU GET THE GOUT, WHICH PUTS YOU IN A PICKLE

MILLY
YOU CATCH A TROUT WITH JUST A LITTLE TICKLE

DOROTHEA/AGNES
WE'VE A SKILL THAT IS SUBLIME

ALL
WE'RE THE FAMOUS SISTERS OF RHYME!

AGNES That was just beginner's luck.

DOROTHEA *This* time you'll be truly stuck.

MILLY Fire away, Ladies!

> **SONG 7a. *"SISTERS OF RHYME"*** – (Encore #1) Milly, Dorothea, Agnes

DOROTHEA
YOU TAKE A FISH AND PUT IT IN YOUR POCKET

MILLY
YOU MAKE A WISH AND FIND A GOLDEN LOCKET

AGNES
YOU PLANT A SEED AND UP COME LOTS OF HOLLYHOCKS

MILLY
YOU HAVE A GREED JUST LIKE THE NAUGHTY GOLDILOCKS

DOROTHEA
YOU PAY A PRICE AND RIDE UPON A LLAMA

MILLY
IT'S AWFULLY NICE, BUT TRAINS ARE SO MUCH CALMER

DOROTHEA/AGNES
WE'VE A SKILL THAT IS SUBLIME

MILLY
AND I DID IT EVERY TIME

ALL
WE'RE THE FAMOUS SISTERS OF RHYME!

MILLY Once more, sisters! But this time *I'll* go first.

SCENE FIVE – REASON AND RHYME

DOROTHEA As you wish.

AGNES Piece of cake!

> ***SONG 7b. "SISTERS OF RHYME"*** – (Encore #2) Milly, Dorothea, Agnes

MILLY
YOU DO A WALTZ AND THEN YOU DO A PLIÉ

DOROTHEA
YOU DO AN UM...

She struggles.
DE DUM DE DUM DE DOO DAH

MILLY
YOU EAT AN ORANGE, AN APPLE AND AN APRICOT

AGNES
YOU EAT AN UM... DE DUM

...oh this is ridiculous, nothing rhymes with orange or apricot. You're too clever for your own good.

DOROTHEA Come along, Agnes, let's leave this revolting child. Now remember what we said, little girl. You must all be gone before dark or it may be too late.

AGNES *(like an echo)* Too late... Too late... Too late...

DOROTHEA You have been warned!

AGNES *(like an echo)* Warned! ...Warned! ...Warned! ...

> **PC GREEN** *enters.*

PC GREEN 'Allo, 'allo, 'allo, what's going on 'ere then?

DOROTHEA Quick, Agnes. It's PC Green. We don't want to get involved.

AGNES *(like an echo)* Involved... Involved... Involved...

They start to exit.

DOROTHEA Be quiet now, dear.

They exit.

PC GREEN And why aren't you in the meadow with your friends, young lady?

MILLY Oh, I...er... I wanted to be on my own to read my book.

PC GREEN *(suspiciously)* I hope you're not up to anything. You shouldn't be talking to strangers.

MILLY Oh, they're harmless. They seem like nice old ladies.

PC GREEN Things are seldom what they seem, my girl. Now come along, I'll take you back to Dumsey Meadow. I'm judging the competition at three o'clock, your friends will be missing you.

MILLY I doubt that very much, PC Green.

Music 7c.

They exit together.

Scene Six – The Battle Begins
Dumsey Meadow

The **VICAR, MR NOBLE, MISS FEATHERSTONE** *and* **CHILDREN** *from both schools (except* **ALEC** *and* **MILLY***) enter from opposite sides and gather in two separate groups, ready for the contest. General excitement as the competitive spirit builds up.* **PERKINS** *is fast asleep on a camping chair throughout the whole scene.*

GERALDINE I think you should know that we Winnies are fully trained in all areas of physical education – you won't stand a chance.

CHILDREN (SW) *(in unison)* Hurrah!

JENNINGS And you should know that St Albert's have won the National Schools Boxing Competition for three years running, so *you* won't stand a chance.

Cheers go up from the **ST ALBERT'S CHILDREN.**

PC GREEN *and* **MILLY** *enter.*

PC GREEN *(to* **MILLY***)* I presume this is your teacher? *(He walks her up to* **MISS FEATHERSTONE.***)*

MISS FEATHERSTONE Millicent Jones, where have you been?

MILLY Nowhere, Miss Featherstone.

MISS FEATHERSTONE "Nowhere" does not exist, Millicent. When we get back to school you will have a lunchtime detention, I shall not forget.

MILLY Yes, Miss Featherstone. Sorry, Miss Featherstone.

MISS FEATHERSTONE And you won't be required for the competition. You will sit quietly somewhere and keep well out of the way.

SYLVIA *(aside to* **GERALDINE***)* No loss there.

MILLY *exits.*

MR NOBLE *(checking off names on his register)* Trussler...yes. Webb...yes. Carter...where's Alec Carter?

JENNINGS He's gone missing, Sir.

MR NOBLE Oh, that wretched boy.

PORTER We don't need him for the competition, Sir. He might be clever, but he's such a weed.

MR NOBLE Thank you, Porter. *(addressing both schools)* Now, as you're aware, we are about to hold a competition to decide which school stays here in Dumsey Meadow. St Albert's, are you ready?

CHILD (SA) *(enthusiastically stepping forward)* St Albert's is the best, best, best,

CHILDREN (SA) Far better than the rest, rest, rest.

The **ST ALBERT'S CHILDREN** *cheer and "roar" as if to scare their opponents.*

MR NOBLE St Winifred's, are you ready?

CHILD (SW) *(enthusiastically stepping forward)* To triumph with ease, you must use the Three C's.

CHILDREN (SW) Courage, Concentration, Commitment. Hurrah!

PORTER *(smugly)* That's actually three "C's" and an "H".

MISS FEATHERSTONE A more refined battle cry, Mr Noble. I think you'll agree.

MR NOBLE We are humbled by your brilliance, Miss Featherstone. *(He gazes rapturously at* **MISS FEATHERSTONE** *for a moment, then breaks away shyly and clears his throat with embarrassment.)* Let the Physical Contest begin!

The **CHILDREN** *prepare for the start of the competition. The* **VICAR, PC GREEN, MR NOBLE** *and* **MISS FEATHERSTONE** *step forward to conduct the proceedings. They are taking it very seriously.*

SCENE SIX – THE BATTLE BEGINS

SONG 8. "THE PHYSICAL CONTEST" – Mr Noble, Miss Featherstone, PC Green, Vicar, Children (not Alec/Milly)

MR NOBLE/MISS F'ST/PC GREEN/VICAR
PREPARE YOURSELVES, THE TIME HAS COME
TO START THE COMPETITION

MR NOBLE
TWO PHYSICAL CHALLENGES – LET'S SEE WHO IS BEST

PC GREEN
AND I WILL BE THE JUDGE
SO WATCH YOUR DISCIPLINE

ALL FOUR
TO ALL OF YOU, GOOD LUCK
AND MAY THE BEST TEAM WIN

Music 8 continues as underscore.

MR NOBLE Physical Challenge number one – a Race around the Meadow. Each school will choose a contestant to run around the circumference of the meadow.

CHILD (SA) What's a circumference, Sir?

MR NOBLE Look it up. You must go round the apple tree in the corner before crossing the finishing line.

The two contestants line up at the start.

PC GREEN Contestants, are you ready? On your marks, get set.

He blows his whistle.

Music 8 continues. The runners race off, which takes them off stage or round the auditorium. The other **CHILDREN** *watch and cheer. Half way round there is a sound effect of a crazy sheep (Effects 9), followed by a scream from the St Albert's Contestant.*

CHILDREN (SA)
COME ON, ST ALBERT'S!

CHILDREN (SW)
　COME ON, ST WINNIE'S!

ALL CHILDREN
　FAST, FAST, DON'T BE LAST
　WE HAVE TO WIN!

Effects 9.

CHILDREN (SA)
　COME ON, ST ALBERT'S!

CHILDREN (SW)
　COME ON, ST WINNIE'S!

ALL CHILDREN
　FAST, FAST, DON'T BE LAST
　WE HAVE TO WIN!

The **ST WINIFRED'S CONTESTANT** *finishes first and the* **ST WINIFRED'S CHILDREN** *cheer. The St Albert's contestant arrives looking slightly dishevelled following the sheep "encounter".*

PC GREEN The winner of the Race around the Meadow is St Winifred's.

ST WINIFRED'S CHILDREN *cheer.* **ST ALBERT'S CHILDREN** *groan disappointedly.*

CHILD (SA) It's not fair, I was attacked by a crazy sheep.

PC GREEN Well, you should have avoided it. You know the animals are a bit peculiar at the moment. I repeat, St Winifred's win the race.

Music 8 continues.

CHILDREN (SW) *(in unison)* Hurrah!

CHILDREN (SW)
　ONE NIL, ONE NIL
　WE'RE LEADING, ONE NIL
　ST WINNIE'S IS WINNING
　IT'S ONE NIL TO US!

SCENE SIX – THE BATTLE BEGINS

GERALDINE Not the "Best, Best, Best" now, are you, St Albert's?

SYLVIA Imagine being attacked by a sheep. You're pathetic.

Music 8 continues as underscore.

MR NOBLE Physical Challenge number two is a Tug of War. All team members will participate and must abide by the rules of the Tug of War Association.

PC GREEN The rope must be less than six inches in circumference—

CHILD (SA) What's a circumference?

PC GREEN Look it up. The rope must be greater than eleven and a half feet in length and free from knots. Remember to pull the rope – anyone found pushing will be disqualified!

The two teams prepare for the Tug of War.

Ready, hold it steady.

He blows his whistle.

The teams pull. A **ST ALBERT'S CHILD** *ties their end of the rope to an immovable object, e.g. the apple tree or the five-bar gate. Nobody notices.*

CHILDREN (SA)
COME ON, ST ALBERT'S

CHILDREN (SW)
COME ON, ST WINNIE'S

ALL CHILDREN
HEAVE-HO, DON'T LET GO
WE HAVE TO WIN!

CHILDREN (SA)
HEAVE!

CHILDREN (SW)
PULL!

CHILDREN (SA)
HO!

CHILDREN (SW)
   PULL!

CHILDREN (SA)
   HEAVE-HO! HEAVE-HO!

CHILDREN (SW)
   AAAAAAARGH!

   The **ST WINIFRED'S CHILDREN** *are pulled over and* **ST ALBERT'S** *win.*

PC GREEN I declare that the winner of the Tug of War is St Albert's and therefore, at the end of the Physical Contest, the score is one all.

JENNINGS Well done, St Albert's. We showed them.

MISS FEATHERSTONE There's still *The Practical Contest* to come, at which St Winifred's will do extremely well, I guarantee. I shall be setting the challenges.

VICAR And I will be the judge.

MISS FEATHERSTONE Let us have a short break, put on our practical hats and prepare for the rest of the competition. Perkins, wake up!

PERKINS *(waking up)* Did I miss something?

MISS FEATHERSTONE Come along, St Winnie's, to work!

   Music 8a. Everyone exits.

Scene Seven – A Meeting of Minds
Somewhere on the Dumsey Estate

MILLY *sits alone, reading the book she was given and making notes.* **ALEC** *enters.*

ALEC Hello.

MILLY Hello.

ALEC I'm Alec.

MILLY I'm Milly.

ALEC So, you're not taking part in the competition either?

MILLY They don't need me. They think I'm clever but weedy.

ALEC That's exactly what my lot say about me.

MILLY Oh, they're just jealous and stupid. Clever people know that being strong isn't everything.

ALEC I quite agree. I can tell you're clever.

MILLY Thanks. I'm not bothered about the competition anyway. I've got a more important challenge. *(proudly)* I'm going to solve *The Mystery of Dumsey Meadow*.

ALEC That's what I'm trying to do. What are your findings so far?

MILLY Extremely interesting, as it happens. I've actually seen the witch and had a very strange encounter with the two old sisters from the village, who try to scare children by speaking in rhyme.

ALEC I don't believe in witches myself, except of course in fairy tales.

MILLY The Sisters of Rhyme believe in fairy tales – and witches. They gave me this book, which has been *very* helpful. What have you found out?

ALEC I've been trailing the farmer and watching his behaviour very closely. I think his animals have the same problem as him. They seem to be singing too!

MILLY I'm sure that between us we can solve this mystery. What do you think?

Music 9 starts as underscore.

ALEC Oh yes, I think we can.

MILLY That would show the others and maybe then they'd start listening to us.

SONG 9. "I'D RATHER HAVE BRAINS THAN BRAWN"
– Alec, Milly

ALEC
PEOPLE WHO SAY THAT A PERSON NEEDS MUSCLES
TO WIN COMPETITIONS AND GET OUT OF TUSSLES
ARE WRONG 'CAUSE THE TRICK IS TO THINK AND BE QUICK
I'D RATHER HAVE BRAINS THAN BRAWN

MILLY
THE HEROES WE WORSHIP ABOVE ALL THE REST
SHOULD NOT BE THE PROUD ONES WHO THINK THEY'RE THE BEST
BUT THE ONES WHO HAVE PASSED AN INTELLIGENCE TEST
I'D RATHER HAVE BRAINS THAN BRAWN

ALEC
IT'S HARD WHEN THE OTHERS IGNORE YOUR IDEAS
AND IT HURTS WHEN THEY TEASE AND MAKE FUN

ALEC/MILLY
BEING DIFFERENT ISN'T EASY
BUT NO MATTER WHAT THEY SAY
WE WILL SHOW THEM, AND THEY'LL KNOW THEN
IT IS BRAINS THAT WIN THE DAY

Music 9 continues as underscore.

SCENE SEVEN – A MEETING OF MINDS

ALEC Take Galileo for example, he was only five foot three, yet he discovered Venus!

MILLY Thomas Edison only weighed eight and a half stone, but he invented the electric light bulb.

ALEC Albert Einstein would never pick a fight, but he discovered that $E = MC^2$.

MILLY And Alexander Graham Bell invented the telephone, thank goodness, but never won a race in his life.

ALEC
> IMAGINE A WORLD WITHOUT ARISTOTLE
> HE WAS BRIGHTER THAN CAESAR

MILLY
> THOUGH CAESAR HAD BOTTLE
> PLATO WAS WISE, HE COULD PHILOSOPHISE

ALEC/MILLY
> I'M GLAD THEY HAD BRAINS NOT BRAWN

MILLY
> ALEXANDER WAS GREAT, BUT HE WASN'T SO CLEVER
> THE EMPIRE HE BUILT IS LOST NOW FOREVER

ALEC (*giving his apple to* **MILLY**)
> BUT NEWTON HAD THEORIES THAT NO ONE CAN SEVER

ALEC/MILLY
> I'M GLAD THEY HAD BRAINS NOT BRAWN

MILLY
> IT'S TRUE THAT THE OTHERS CAN MAKE YOU FEEL SMALL
> WHEN YOU TRY TO CONVINCE THEM YOU'RE RIGHT

ALEC/MILLY
> BEING DIFFERENT ISN'T EASY
> BUT NO MATTER WHAT THEY SAY
> WE WILL SHOW THEM, AND THEY'LL KNOW THEN
> IT IS BRAINS THAT WIN THE DAY
> BEING DIFFERENT ISN'T EASY
> BUT NO MATTER WHAT THEY SAY

WE WILL SHOW THEM, AND THEY'LL KNOW THEN
IT IS BRAINS THAT WIN THE DAY
IT IS BRAINS NOT BRAWN THAT WIN IN EVERY WAY

ALEC Right. I've got some questions for that singing farmer.

MILLY Good. And I need to find the Sisters of Rhyme. I've something important to tell them.

ALEC This is fun. We're solving the mystery together.

MILLY *(pause)* I'm glad you're my friend, Alec.

ALEC *(thinking for a second, then changing the subject)* Best of luck, Milly.

MILLY Thanks.

They go to exit in different directions.

ALEC Oh and Milly...

MILLY Yes, Alec?

ALEC ...I'm glad you're my friend too.

They both smile and exit.

Music 10 starts.

Scene Eight – War and Peace
Dumsey Meadow

The CHILDREN from both schools (except ALEC and MILLY) enter from opposite sides and gather in two separate groups ready for the Practical Contest. General excitement as the competitive spirit builds up again.

SYLVIA *(to GERALDINE)* I wonder what practical challenges Miss Featherstone will ask us to do.

GERALDINE Don't worry, I'm sure it will be things she knows we're good at, *(winking)* if you know what I mean.

PORTER *(worriedly)* Jennings, I think they're up to something. If we're not careful, *we'll* be the ones going home.

JENNINGS Don't worry, keep your wits about you and use your initiative, *(winking)* if you know what I mean.

CHILD (SW) Here they come!

Music 10 continues.

The **VICAR, PC GREEN, MR NOBLE** *and* **MISS FEATHERSTONE** *enter ceremoniously.*

SONG 10. "THE PRACTICAL CONTEST" – Miss Featherstone, Mr Noble, Vicar, PC Green, Geraldine, Jennings, Children (not Alec/Milly)

MISS FEATHERSTONE/MR NOBLE/VICAR/PC GREEN
PREPARE YOURSELVES TO CARRY ON
AND CONCLUDE THIS COMPETITION

MISS FEATHERSTONE
TWO PRACTICAL CHALLENGES TO DECIDE WHO WILL STAY

VICAR
AND I WILL BE THE JUDGE
FOR CHEATING IS A SIN

ALL FOUR
> TO ALL OF YOU GOOD LUCK
> AND MAY THE BEST TEAM WIN!

Music 10 continues as underscore.

MISS FEATHERSTONE Practical Challenge number one – Singing a Camping Song. *(winking conspiratorially at the* **ST WINIFRED'S CHILDREN***)* Each team will select a soloist and form a choir. Points will be awarded for melodic inventiveness, counterpoint and harmonic modulation.

PORTER You what?!

VICAR How wonderful, I'm looking forward to this one. St Winifred's School, you may go first. *(overenthusiastically)* A-one, a-two, a-one, two, three, four.

He tinkles his bell.

GERALDINE
> A TIME TO LEARN, A TIME TO LIVE
> A CHANCE TO PLAY, A CHANCE TO GIVE
> A CHALLENGE FOR US ALL TO FACE
> TO GIVE IN WOULD BE SUCH DISGRACE

CHILDREN (SW)
> WITH CHIN HELD HIGH THROUGH SUN AND RAIN
> OUR SPIRIT SHALL NOT WAIVER
> THE TENT MAY LEAK, BUT DON'T COMPLAIN
> AND BE KIND TO YOUR NEIGHBOUR

VICAR Congratulations St Winifred's – you should all be in the Dumsey Church Choir – they could do with some help. Your turn, St Albert's.

PORTER *(aside to* **JENNINGS***)* What are we going to do?

JENNINGS It'll be fine. We'll do what they did, just follow my lead.

***JENNINGS** assumes a "mock" choirboy stance. The others copy him.*

ST ALBERT'S IS THE BEST, BEST, BEST

CHILDREN (SA)
FAR BETTER THAN THE REST, REST, REST

JENNINGS
ST ALBERT'S SCHOOL IS GREAT, GREAT, GREAT

CHILDREN (SA)
COMPARED TO US YOU'RE SECOND-RATE

JENNINGS
WE'RE THE BEST

CHILDREN (SA)
WE'RE THE BEST

JENNINGS
SO PBBT* TO THE REST

He blows a raspberry.

CHILDREN (SA)
ST ALBERT'S IS THE BETTER

JENNINGS
WE ARE GREAT

CHILDREN (SA)
WE ARE GREAT

JENNINGS
ST ALBERT'S IS GREAT

JENNINGS/CHILDREN
ST WINIFRED'S IS WETTER!

VICAR Well, what an unusual performance! It would raise a few eyebrows in church, I must say. And a good thing too, they could do with a kick up the aisle! The winner of the Singing a Camping song contest is...

Music 10 continues as underscore.

...St Albert's!

The ST ALBERT'S CHILDREN *cheer, the* ST WINIFRED'S CHILDREN *groan.*

CHILDREN (SA)
TWO ONE, TWO ONE
WE'RE LEADING, TWO ONE
ST ALBERT'S IS WINNING
IT'S TWO ONE TO US!

CHILD (SW) If we lose the next one, they'll be staying.

CHILD (SW) And Perkins will have to drive us all home.

CHILD (SA) Yes. You might as well save time and leave now.

PERKINS *(entering)* Did someone call? Are we off? I'll get the bus round.

MISS FEATHERSTONE It's not over yet. We will give our all until the bitter end. Isn't that right, children?

The ST WINIFRED'S CHILDREN *cheer.*

MR NOBLE *(determined)* Right. *(with confidence)* Until the bitter end... *(he struggles to think of something original)* we will give our all.

Music 10 continues as underscore.

The ST ALBERT'S CHILDREN *groan at his pathetic attempt.*

MISS FEATHERSTONE And so, to the final challenge – Building a Campfire. Each team should work together on the construction. This can be in the style of your choice, but must be suitable for boiling a pan of water.

GERALDINE *(aside)* Did you clear away all the twigs like I told you to?

SYLVIA Yes, not a twig or stick in sight.

VICAR Good luck with this one, it shouldn't be difficult. Here we go, ready, aim and campfire!

He tinkles his bell.

Music 10 continues.

During the song, the **ST WINIFRED'S CHILDREN** *produce a table with tablecloth, camping stove with pan of water or kettle and a tea service on a tray. This is all done with true St Winifred's style, grace and precision. The* **ST ALBERT'S CHILDREN** *run around vainly looking for twigs but only succeed in finding one.*

CHILDREN (SA)
COME ON, ST ALBERT'S!

CHILDREN (SW)
COME ON, ST WINNIE'S!

ALL CHILDREN
QUICK, QUICK, FIND A STICK
GATHER THEM IN!

CHILDREN (SA)
COME ON, ST ALBERT'S!

CHILDREN (SW)
COME ON, ST WINNIE'S!

ALL CHILDREN
FIRE, FIRE, MUSTN'T TIRE
WE HAVE TO WIN!

VICAR Well, I'm flabbergasted! Not a campfire in sight. *(picking up the St Albert's solitary twig)* What use is this?

PORTER It's not our fault. We searched for more but there weren't any.

The **ST WINIFRED'S CHILDREN** *snigger nastily.*

VICAR *(examining the* **ST WINIFRED'S CHILDREN**'s *work)* And what is the meaning of this?

GERALDINE Miss Featherstone said, and I quote, "Each team should work together to construct a fire".

SYLVIA Which we did.

GERALDINE And that it could be "In the style of your choice but must be suitable for boiling a pan of water".

SYLVIA Which ours is.

VICAR Well now. We must have a winner and in view of the circumstances—

CHILD (SA) What's a circumstance?

EVERYONE Look it up!

VICAR *(pointedly at the child who interrupted)* In view of the circumstances – St Winifred's win the point for using their initiative.

The **ST WINIFRED'S CHILDREN** *cheer, the* **ST ALBERT'S CHILDREN** *boo.*

MISS FEATHERSTONE So that means it is a draw, two points each.

LADY DUMSEY *and the* **JOURNALIST** *enter.* **LADY DUMSEY** *is counting the money she has been paid for the interview.*

LADY DUMSEY *(putting the money into her pocket)* Well, that's marvellous, Mr Fleet. Many thanks for your time... *(aside)* and the money.

JOURNALIST And thank *you* for your exclusive interview on the Dumsey witch. People will be queuing for miles to buy tomorrow's *Daily Herald*.

LADY DUMSEY *attracts the attention of the* **CHILDREN**, **MR NOBLE** *and* **MISS FEATHERSTONE**. *The* **JOURNALIST** *takes a keen interest and makes notes throughout the scene.*

LADY DUMSEY Good afternoon, everyone. Have you decided which school is going to stay?

PC GREEN The competition was a dead heat, Lady Dumsey.

SCENE EIGHT – WAR AND PEACE

LADY DUMSEY Well, that's no good. I told you, if you can't decide, you'll all have to leave.

VICAR Hold on a mo, what we need is a tie-break.

LADY DUMSEY *(mishearing the VICAR)* A *tea*-break, what a good idea, Vicar. After all, it is four o'clock.

MR NOBLE But we should sort it out now, Lady Dumsey. There's no time for tea.

VICAR Why not make the tea-break the tie-break?

LADY DUMSEY Jolly good idea, Vicar. Each school will produce a cup of tea and bring it to me – the best-tasting tea will win and that school can stay.

JENNINGS That's not fair, we haven't got a campfire.

VICAR *(emphatically)* Improvise. PC Green, would you care to start them off?

PC GREEN With pleasure. Right, tea for Lady D! On your marks, get set.

He blows his whistle.

SONG 10a. "THE TEA-BREAK TIE-BREAK" – Children (not Alec/Milly)

The **ST ALBERT'S CHILDREN** *look around in vain, wondering what to do, while the* **ST WINIFRED'S CHILDREN** *casually make their tea.*

CHILDREN (SA)
COME ON, ST ALBERT'S!

CHILDREN (SW)
COME ON, ST WINNIE'S!

ALL CHILDREN
TEA, TEA, MAKE THE TEA—

They are interrupted by the sound of the **FARMER** *and* **ALEC** *singing offstage, everyone stops to listen.*

SONG 10b. "THE GLADNESS OF THE MAY" – (Reprise)
Farmer Bill, Alec

FARMER BILL/ALEC
THE SUN HAS RISEN ON A BRIGHT NEW DAY
MY HEART IS FULL OF JOY

The **FARMER** *and* **ALEC** *enter, they are very jolly. The* **FARMER** *is carrying his flask of tea.*
I'D LIKE TO SKIP AND RUN AND PLAY
AND FEEL "THE GLADNESS OF THE MAY!"
JUST LIKE A LOVESICK BOY

MR NOBLE Alec Carter, where have you been? I don't remember giving you permission to wander off.

ALEC I know, Sir. Sorry, Sir. But I've been doing some very important research.

LADY DUMSEY Farmer Bill, I thought I instructed you to get on with your work.

FARMER BILL Indeed, Ma'am, but I'm just going for my tea break. Young Alec here is joining me.

JENNINGS It pains me to say this, Carter, but you're a genius. *(snatching the flask from* **FARMER BILL***)* Give us that flask. *(he pours tea into the cup and offers it to* **LADY DUMSEY***)* There you are, Lady Dumsey, a cup of tea.

GERALDINE But that's the Farmer's tea, you didn't make it.

JENNINGS *(mimicking* **GERALDINE***)* Lady Dumsey said, and I quote, "Each school will produce a cup of tea".

PORTER Which we did.

JENNINGS "And bring it to me".

PORTER Which we have.

VICAR Well, it should be allowed then. You asked for two cups of tea, Lady Dumsey, and here they are.

LADY DUMSEY Fair enough, let's get on with it, I'm parched. I shall try this one first.

She sips the St Winifred's tea.

Hmmn, that tastes delicious. And now this one.

She sips the flask tea but struggles to swallow it.

(*spitting out the tea*) Dear me, that really isn't very nice at all. I declare the St Winifred's tea to be superior.

The **ST WINIFRED'S CHILDREN** *cheer and are delighted with their victory.*

(*returning to the St Albert's cup and taking another sip*) On second thoughts...this tea has a sweet, strangely familiar and not altogether unpleasant taste. It reminds me of something. Where did the water come from?

ALEC From the well in the orchard. Isn't that right, Farmer Bill?

FARMER BILL That's right.

ALEC He gets all his water from the well.

LADY DUMSEY (*asking the* **ST WINIFRED'S CHILD**) And yours?

GERALDINE From the stream.

LADY DUMSEY Farmer Bill, you are in charge of the well. What's going on?

FARMER BILL I don't know, Ma'am. I thought the water tasted a bit odd lately, but I never said nothing 'cause the animals weren't complaining.

PC GREEN So do you drink the same water as you give your animals?

ALEC (*jumping in*) Yes, he does. And his wife drinks it too.

FARMER BILL It's never done us any harm.

ALEC (*emphatically*) Oh, but it has!

MISS FEATHERSTONE Control that boy, Mr Noble. He's caused enough trouble as it is.

MR NOBLE No, let's give Alec one last chance.

MISS FEATHERSTONE *(to* **ALEC***)* Well...?!

ALEC The strange smell, the crazy animals and the singing farmer can all be explained. Farmer Bill put all the bad apples from the failed harvest in a large pile next to the well where they rotted down. This seeped into the ground, entered the water table and ended up in the well. Without oxygen, a process known as fermentation started and without knowing it, what they've all been drinking is C_2H_5OH – or to put it another way – alcohol.

VICAR So what we can smell is...

ALEC Cider!

PERKINS Cider? Now you're talking!

LADY DUMSEY I knew I recognised it!

PC GREEN So, the farmer, his wife and all the animals are...

ALEC Drunk!

FARMER BILL Well, I'll be... *(hiccoughs)* sorry.

LADY DUMSEY Congratulations, young man. How jolly clever of you to solve the mystery.

MR NOBLE You've done us all proud, Alec. Well done.

JENNINGS What a surprise! Didn't think you had it in you, Carter.

Offers his hand to **ALEC** *and they shake.*

PC GREEN That's one mystery explained, but what about the witch?

The **ELDERLY SISTERS** *enter, with* **MILLY** *hidden behind them.* **MILLY** *is dressed to look like them and is using a walking stick.*

SCENE EIGHT – WAR AND PEACE

DOROTHEA We told you all to go away,
 We said it wasn't safe to stay.

AGNES The children will get such a fright
 When the witch appears at dead of night.

CHILD (SA) Why don't you stop trying to scare us?

*The **ELDERLY SISTERS** part, revealing **MILLY** behind them. She steps forward and mimics the **SISTERS**.*

MILLY Go now, before it's much too late,
 Before the witch has sealed your fate.

GERALDINE Not you as well, Milly.

ALEC Leave her alone, she knows what she's doing.

Music 10c.

*There is a loud, manic cackle (Effects 10) and the **HOODED WOMAN** appears. Everyone except **MILLY** is terrified.*

MILLY *(herself again)* There's no need to be scared everyone, witches don't exist.

***MILLY** holds up the book of fairy tales.*

MILLY/ALEC Except in fairy tales.

They look at each other.

*She walks up to the **HOODED WOMAN**.*

LADY DUMSEY Child, be careful! Stop her! Don't go near the witch!

MILLY Ladies and Gentlemen, may I present...

*She removes the cloak boldly from the **HOODED WOMAN**'s head. There is a gasp from the crowd.*

PC GREEN Goodness me. It's the Vicar's wife!

VICAR Mary! You're meant to be in a clinic in Bracklesea!

MARY Quick, Virginia, the game's up. Let's make a run for it!

Music 10d.

The **HOODED WOMAN** *and* **LADY DUMSEY** *start to run but the* **CHILDREN** *surround and trap them. The* **JOURNALIST** *is eagerly taking photographs.*

PC GREEN Stand back please, everyone. Stand back. I'm going to have to ask a few questions. Millicent, do you have an explanation?

MILLY Yes, Sir. Lady Dumsey invented the witch so that she could sell the story to the newspaper – I heard her discussing the fee with the journalist.

ALEC Well done, Milly. You clever thing.

MILLY And she asked the Vicar's wife to be the witch.

VICAR Mary, is this true?

MARY Yes, and we would have got away with it if it wasn't for this meddling child.

PC GREEN I'm going to have to arrest you both and take you down to the station for questioning.

LADY DUMSEY Please don't. I was in desperate need of money after the failed apple harvest. I'm terribly sorry, really I am.

JOURNALIST The money please, Lady Dumsey. We won't be running the story after all.

LADY DUMSEY *takes the money out of her pocket and gives it to the* **JOURNALIST**.

Thank you. But I can see a new headline – "Lady Dumsey and Vicar's Wife in Get Witch Quick Trick!"

MARY It wasn't my fault. Lady Dumsey *made* me do it.

LADY DUMSEY *(defensively)* Yes, but you were getting half the money.

SCENE EIGHT – WAR AND PEACE

MARY *(desperately)* Look, if you let us off, I'll make you enough jam to last the whole year.

LADY DUMSEY *(persuasively)* You *know* how much you like Mary's jam, PC Green.

ALEC Bribing an officer of the law—

MILLY Inventing a witch—

ALEC Lying to a national newspaper.

MILLY/ALEC You'll go to prison for that.

PC GREEN Well...I am rather partial to your strawberry jam, Mary. *(pause)* Very well, how can I refuse?

A gasp of surprise from the crowd and relief from **LADY DUMSEY** *and* **MARY**.

VICAR How did you know Mary was the witch, Milly?

MILLY I overheard you speaking to Lady Dumsey about your wife's illness. I simply telephoned all the clinics in Bracklesea and none of them had a Mary in their care. I heard Lady Dumsey say that Mary was a good pantomime actress and I simply put two and two together.

MISS FEATHERSTONE I'm impressed, Millicent. I can see we've got a Head Girl in the making.

GERALDINE Well done. *(offering her hand)* I didn't think you had it in you.

They shake hands.

DOROTHEA *(aside to* **AGNES***)* Sister, we should have known it was Mary all along. Her acting is unmistakeably awful.

AGNES Terribly wooden.

MR NOBLE What I don't understand is why you two ladies tried to scare us so much.

ALL CHILDREN Yes!

DOROTHEA We didn't want silly children around...

AGNES ...so we used the witch as an excuse to try and make you leave.

JENNINGS What a cheek!

GERALDINE That was jolly rotten of you.

DOROTHEA Yes it was. But when our little friend told us the witch was Mary...

AGNES ...we realised just how clever children can be...

DOROTHEA ...and we changed our minds. But as for you Lady Dumsey—

DOROTHEA/AGNES We're appalled!

The crowd agree.

MISS FEATHERSTONE Look, the lady has apologised, let's all forgive and forget. At St Winifred's we don't bear grudges, do we children?

CHILDREN (SW) We don't bear grudges.

MR NOBLE Miss Featherstone, you are an inspiration. I've learnt so much from you. *(proudly)* St Albert's, tell them our new motto.

CHILDREN (SA) Civis Romanus sum!

[si-viss ro-mah-noos soom]

MR NOBLE Which means, in translation?

CHILD (SA) I am a Roman citizen.

MISS FEATHERSTONE looks at MR NOBLE with a wry smile.

MR NOBLE It needs work!

MILLY Well, I think we should all be friends now. Don't you?

VICAR Good idea, Milly. Come on chaps. "Friends are better than foes, as everyone knows".

He laughs at his rhyme.

SCENE EIGHT - WAR AND PEACE

The CHILDREN *mingle and acknowledge each other in a friendly way for the first time.*

MR NOBLE *offers* MISS FEATHERSTONE *his hand.*

MR NOBLE Friends, Miss Featherstone?

MISS FEATHERSTONE *(offering her hand)* Oh, call me Felicity.

MR NOBLE *takes her hand and kisses it.*

Oh, Kenneth.

PC GREEN This is all very well, but we still have a problem. Which school will be staying in Dumsey Meadow?

GERALDINE Well, it's clear to me that we should *all* stay, especially... *(she looks at* JENNINGS *coyly)* as we're all friends now... *(she grabs* JENNINGS' *hand, which embarrasses him)*

LADY DUMSEY I told you before, you can't all stay. There's not enough room.

JENNINGS Come on, Lady D. You owe us one. We're all staying.

ALL CHILDREN We're staying!

LADY DUMSEY But where?

SYLVIA St Winnie's could camp on your croquet lawn!

PORTER Nice one, Sylvia, that'll teach her!

LADY DUMSEY My precious croquet lawn! Your tents will ruin it!

PERKINS Too bad! And you can help put them up.

Pause. They all turn to stare at LADY DUMSEY.

LADY DUMSEY Oh very well then. *(Music 11 starts as underscore.)* Use my croquet lawn, use my meadow, use my house – it's all yours!

Everyone cheers.

SONG 11. "HOW THRILLING!" – (Reprise #2) Company
I'M SORRY FOR THE THINGS I'VE DONE

    MY WORDS ARE MOST SINCERE
    I'VE CAUSED A LOT OF TROUBLE
    IT WAS A SILLY THING TO DO

MARY (*spoken*) AND I AM SORRY TOO!

DOROTHEA/AGNES (*sung*)
    WE APOLOGISE FOR BEING GLUM
    WE'RE GLAD THAT YOU ARE HERE

PC GREEN
    MY HEART WITH JOY IS FILLING

VICAR (*spoken*) OH IT REALLY IS SO ABSOLUTELY THRILLING!

COMPANY
    HOW THRILLING
    HOW THRILLING
    IT REALLY IS SO ABSOLUTELY THRILLING
    EXCITING!
    INVITING!

CHILDREN
    A CAMPING TRIP FOR FIVE WHOLE DAYS
    WE'LL HAVE SUCH FUN

LADY DUMSEY (*spoken*) AND NO ONE PAYS!

COMPANY (*sung*)
    HOW SPIFFING
    HOW RIPPING
    ONE COULD REMARK THIS CAMPING LARK IS GRIPPING

CHILDREN (SA)
    HOORAY FOR ALEC, HE'S THE BEST
    HE PUT HIS TALENTS TO THE TEST

CHILDREN (SW)
    HURRAH, HURRAH FOR MILLY TOO
    SHE SHOWED US ALL WHAT SHE COULD DO

ALEC/MILLY
    AS WORDSWORTH AND THE FARMER SAY
    LET'S "FEEL THE GLADNESS OF THE MAY"!

SCENE EIGHT - WAR AND PEACE

COMPANY
>IT REALLY, REALLY, REALLY IS
>IT REALLY, REALLY, REALLY IS
>IT REALLY, REALLY, REALLY IS
>IT REALLY, REALLY, REALLY IS
>IT REALLY, REALLY, REALLY, REALLY,
>REALLY, REALLY, REALLY IS...

ALEC I've just had a thought...

COMPANY *(slightly annoyed)* What?!

ALEC We've discovered who the witch was and solved the mystery of the water from the well...

ALL *(curiously)* Well...?!

ALEC ...but what this doesn't explain is...

ALL *(impatiently)* Is...?!

ALEC *(dramatically)* Why *did* the apple harvest fail?

>*Music 11 continues. There is a flash of lightning and a different cackle is heard – bigger and more frightening than before (Effects 11). They all gasp and freeze in horror.*

>*Blackout.*

>***SONG 11a. "BOWS"*** *–* (Encore) Company

COMPANY
>WE LIKE TO SING A JOLLY SONG
>WE WANT THE WORLD TO SING ALONG
>AND WHEN WE SING, SUCH JOY WE BRING
>FOR SINGING IS A HAPPY THING

GROUP 1
>WE LIKE TO SING

GROUP 2
>...WE LIKE TO SING

GROUP 1
>A JOLLY SONG

GROUP 2
...A JOLLY SONG

GROUP 1
WE WANT THE WORLD

GROUP 2
...WE WANT THE WORLD

GROUP 1
TO SING ALONG

GROUP 2
...TO SING ALONG

GROUP 1
AND WHEN WE SING

GROUP 2
...AND WHEN WE SING

GROUP 1
SUCH JOY WE BRING

GROUP 2
...SUCH JOY WE BRING

GROUP 1
FA LA LA LA

GROUP 2
...FA LA LA LA

GROUP 1
FA LA LA LA

GROUP 2
...FA LA LA LA

COMPANY
FOR SINGING... IS A JOLLY HAPPY THING!

Music 11b.

The **COMPANY** *and the audience exit.*

EXTRA DIALOGUE FOR CHILDREN

If it is considered necessary to give more lines of dialogue to St Albert's and St Winifred's Children, then the following idea can be used. Before the start of the play, i.e. before the Prologue (page 1), children from each school could enter, individually or in groups, and read out entries from their diaries. This would be a good way of introducing the Children, the adventure they are about to embark upon and, more comically perhaps, the differences between the schools. Some jolly 1930s music could be playing in the background to help evoke the period. They should be positioned far downstage and lit separately if possible so as not to appear part of the set. Examples of dialogue:

CHILD (SW) Dear Diary, I can't wait to go to Dumsey Meadow – I've never been camping before. I wonder what it's like? I'm really excited!

CHILD (SA) Dear Diary, We're going to Dumsey Meadow tomorrow on a boring camping trip. I hate the countryside – nothing ever happens there!

CHILD (SW) Dear Diary, I hope we see lots of beautiful flowers in the meadow. Flowers are so pretty – I can't wait to smell them.

CHILD (SA) I hope there aren't too many flowers, or any at all – they smell disgusting!

CHILD (SW) Dear Diary, I'm not going near any of the animals, they're so dirty – but I'm still looking forward to going.

CHILD (SA) I hope there are some animals in Dumsey Meadow – pigs would be best.

Later in the play, at the suggested interval point (page 44), before the start of the second half, there could be another moment for the schoolchildren to do a similar thing. On this occasion they could be writing home to their parents, commenting on the events of the first half and once again emphasising their differences. Examples of dialogue:

CHILD (SW) Dear Mother and Father, Being in Dumsey Meadow is wonderful but we have a slight problem – St Albert's school is intending to stay here as well. It's a boy's school and there are a lot of boys, but I'm not complaining about that! Love Sylvia

CHILD (SA) Dear Mum and Dad, I hate it here, it smells, and there are lots of girls – yuk! Love George

CHILD (SW) Dear Mother, Camping is fun! But the campsite has been doublebooked by Lady Dumsey. It sounds like she has a lot on her plate, poor thing. Anyway, we're having a competition to see who will be staying. I know it'll be us! Love Betty

CHILD (SA) Dear Mum, Some awful posh girl's school wants to camp here too so we're having a competition to see who will be staying – they don't stand a chance! Missing you – sort of, Tom. P.S. don't expect any more letters.

PLEASE NOTE: **If extra dialogue is being added in this way, then the following should appear on the poster or in the programme:**

"Diary entries and letters home written by members of the cast"

FURNITURE AND PROPERTY LIST

Wherever possible the items mentioned below should evoke the period in which this play is set, i.e. the 1930s. Further properties may be added at the director's discretion.

Onstage: Small branch/twig (**Alec**)

Offstage: Thermos flask (**Farmer Bill**)
Rucksack and map (**Miss Featherstone**)
Tents, rucksacks, camping equipment including a camping chair (**Perkins**)
Tents, rucksacks, camping equipment (**Children SA**)
Newspaper cutting, register (**Mr Noble**)
Spectacles, map, satchel containing an apple, notebook and pencil (**Alec**)
Shotgun, long piece of paper with list of things to do, a healthy "wodge" of bank notes (**Lady Dumsey**)
Walking sticks, an old book (**Dorothea and Agnes**)
Truncheon, whistle, long rope for tug-of-war (**PC Green**)
Old-fashioned camera, notepad (**Journalist**)
Hockey/Lacrosse sticks, Tennis/Badminton racquets etc. (**Children SW**)
Satchel containing notebook and pencil, walking stick (**Milly**)
Small bell (**Vicar**)
A small camping table with tablecloth, camping stove with pan of water or kettle and a tea service on a tray (**Children SW**)

SOUND EFFECTS PLOT

Specially recorded sound effects can be obtained from Samuel French Ltd

Effects 1   Atmosphere track, played during pre-set as audience arrives, fading as the **Farmer** starts singing   (page 1)

Effects 2   **Farmer Bill:** "Till evening comes along"   (page 2)
Crazy cow mooing

Effects 3   **Farmer Bill:** "Just like a love-sick boy"   (page 2)
Crazy sheep bah-ing

Effects 4   **Farmer Bill:** "The sun has risen on a bright new day, the..."   (page 2)
Witch-like cackle

Effects 5   **Lady Dumsey** enters and points her gun into the air   (page 11)
Gunshot

Effects 6   **Lady Dumsey:** "Would somebody care to explain" The children all start to shout at once. She points her gun into the air   (page 11)
Gunshot

Effects 7   During Music 3b on a music/visual cue   (page 21)
Witch-like cackle

Effects 8   End of Song 4. **All:** "So beware!"   (page 31)
Witch-like cackle

Effects 9   **All Children:** "We have to win" (during race around the meadow)   (page 55)
Crazy sheep bah-ing

Effects 10   **Alec:** "Leave her alone, she knows what she's doing"   (page 73)
Witch-like cackle

Effects 11 **Alec:** "Why did the apple harvest fail?" (page 79)
Witch-like cackle with lightning and thunder

BACKING TRACK PLOT

If live music is not an option, specially recorded backing tracks can be obtained from Samuel French Ltd. Please note that the backing tracks *include* the sound effects as mentioned throughout the script.

Track	Cue	Music/Effects	Page
1	Play as audience arrives. Fade on clearance	Effects 1	1
2	On clearance (includes Effects 2, 3 and 4)	1	
3	As Farmer Bill exits	2 (i)	2
4	*Thank you Sylvia, I didn't*	2 (ii)	5
5	*Adventure is the essence of life and fortune favours the bold, Miss Featherstone*	2 (iii)	6
6	*Carter smells! Carter smells!*	2b	8
7	Lady Dumsey enters and fires her shotgun	Effects 5	11
8	Lady Dumsey fires her shotgun again	Effects 6	11
9	*Be quiet, Milly!*	3	12
10	*Geraldine, you're in charge*	3a	18
11	Start of Scene Two (includes Effects 7)	3b	21
12	*Agreed!*	3c	24
13	*Maybe she's come back to haunt the meadow* (includes Effects 8)	4	27
14	*Maybe we'll catch the witch for you*	5	33
15	*Off we go, left, right, left, right, left, right*	5a	37
16	*Can't you see how much work there is to do?*	6	40
17	*...oh yes, that was important...*	6a (i)	45

18	If there is an interval, play this track before the start of the second half. Jump to track 19 if there is no interval	6a (ii)	45
19	*Of course, we are the Sisters of Rhyme!*	7(i)	47
20	*Ready when you are.*	7(ii)	49
21	*Fire away, Ladies!*	7a	50
22	*Piece of cake!*	7b	51
23	*I doubt that very much, PC Green!*	7c	52
24	*Let the Physical Contest begin!* (includes Effects 9)	8 (i)	54
25	*I repeat, St Winifred's win the race*	8 (ii)	56
26	*You're pathetic*	8 (iii)	57
27	*Come along, St Winnie's, to work!*	8a	58
28	*I'm sure that between us we can solve this mystery. What do you think?*	9	60
29	Milly and Alec exit. (Start of Scene Eight) Fade on dialogue	10 (i)	62
30	*Here they come! (stop on:* St Winifred's School, you may go first*)*	10 (ii)	63
31	*A-one, a-two, a-one, two, three, four*	10 (iii)	64
32	*Just follow my lead*	10 (iv)	64
33	*The winner of the Singing Camping Song is...*	10 (v)	65
34	*...we will give our all*	10 (vi)	66
35	*On your marks, get set (whistle)*	10a : 10b	69
36	*Leave her alone, she knows what she's doing* (includes Effects 10)	10c	73
37	*Let's make a run for it!*	10d	74
38	*Oh, very well then*	11 (i)	77
39	*Why did the apple harvest fail?* (includes Effects 11)	11 (ii)	79

| 40 | On lights up for bows | 11a | 79 |
| 41 | During applause after previous track | 11b | 80 |

THIS IS NOT THE END

**Visit samuelfrench.co.uk
and discover the best
theatre bookshop
on the internet**

A vast range of plays
Acting and theatre books
Gifts

samuelfrench.co.uk

samuelfrenchltd

samuel french uk